SWEET NOTHINGS

Over 50 Luscious, Low Fat, Low Calorie Desserts

BY

Jill O'Connor

~

PHOTOGRAPHY

Susan Marie Anderson

~

CHRONICLE BOOKS

SAN FRANCISCO

Text Copyright © 1993 by Jill O'Connor.

Photographs Copyright © 1993 by Susan
Marie Anderson.

Design by Sandra McHenry.

Editing by Sharon Silva.

Food Styling by Jill O'Connor.

Composition by On Line Typography.

Library of Congress Cataloging-in-
Publication Data

O'Connor, Jill.
Sweet nothings : over 50 luscious, low fat,
low calorie desserts / by Jill O'Connor :
photography by Susan Marie Anderson.
p. cm.
ISBN 0-8118-0289-2 (pbk)
1. Desserts. 2. Low-fat diet—Recipes. I.
Title.
TX773.032 1993
641.8'6—dc20   92-25616
                                 CIP

Printed in Japan.

Distributed in Canada by Raincoast Books,
112 East Third Ave.,
Vancouver, B.C. V5T 1C8

10 9 8 7 6 5 4 3 2

Chronicle Books
275 Fifth Street
San Francisco, CA 94103

Acknowledgments

My sincere appreciation to the following people for their gracious contributions:

Sheri Shansby Boyden, registered dietician with the Mayo Clinic in Rochester, Minnesota, and good friend, for her sound advice and assistance with the nutritional analysis.

Ariann and Peggy at the elegant Best of All Worlds shop in Seattle, for the beautiful and luxurious items that grace the photographs.

Rocky and Pia at Inside, a stunning emporium in Seattle, for their wonderful and unique contributions to these pages.

Viki at Miss Hattie's Art Antiques and Unusual Goods on Bainbridge Island, Washington, for the lovely peach lusterware tea set and antique kitchenware.

Gretchen Bennett for her beautiful hand-painted linens and backgrounds.

Anna Bak Kvapil for her lovely painted background.

Pilchuck glass artists John T. McComish and John Frank Englesby for the beautiful goblets.

De Medici Ming Fine Paper, Seattle, for the Italian marbled paper backgrounds.

Dick Bowen for his public beach access and trail on Bainbridge Island, Washington.

Nancy and Chester Bennett and George and Mary Anderson for the use of family china, silver and linens.

Ken Bennett for his assistance and helpful advice with the photography.

Barbara Stetson for the lovely Quimper ware dishes and for listening.

Robert and Carole Reek for searching out the perfect apricot branches in the middle of winter and for sending them overnight from California to Washington, and for their love and continued excitement and interest about every detail of this book.

James O'Connor for his loving support and enthusiasm throughout the course of this project.

Adam and Seth—just because.

Bill LeBlond and Leslie Jonath for believing in this project from the very beginning and helping me through.

My family and friends for their encouragement and heartfelt good wishes for success with this book.

*To my mother and
father for always
reminding me that
"We are so very proud
of you"; and especially
to Jim for helping me
make all my dreams
come true.*

~

Contents

SWEET NOTHINGS

{ INTRODUCTION }

The stove, the bins, the cupboards, I had learned forever, make an inviolable throne room. From there I ruled; temporarily I controlled. I felt powerful, and I loved that feeling. ~ M. F. K. FISHER, "THE GASTRONOMICAL ME," IN *THE ART OF EATING*

During the summers after my sophomore and junior years in college, I worked as a cook at a small, family-run resort in California's Trinity Alps. The kitchen manager, a family friend and an eternally optimistic employer, hired me with no experience cooking for a group larger— and less forgiving—than my family. I arrived a twenty-year-old neophyte, armed with the spirit of Fannie Farmer, Julia Child, and Maida Heatter to guide me.

~My first big night bordered on complete disaster; cooking for fifty held perils unknown for someone who had never cooked for more than five. The hash browns I had envisioned as crisp and tender were instead charred and mushy. The sautéed mushrooms resembled bits of shriveled leather and the Caesar salad was slimy

with eggs that, in my panic, I had forgotten to coddle. I was relieved the guests were barbecuing their own steaks! Wobbly with exhaustion and frustration, I served the final course with grim determination: a fresh strawberry-ice cream pie in a dark chocolate cookie crust, smothered with thick hot fudge and mounds of whipped cream. The sighs of pleasure drifting from the dining room into the kitchen warmed my heart and helped me forget my aching feet. I was hooked. Since that day my forays into a professional kitchen have met with better results, and I decided then and there to stick with the area of my first real success— desserts.

~What is it about desserts that captures people's devotion? Why are sweets so delectable to the human palate? Eating is one of the great sensual pleasures of life, and many of us enjoy desserts as we might

a secret lover; savoring them discreetly— a furtive indulgence with more than a little guilt attached. Although some people are satisfied with an occasional sweet treat, there are many for whom cheesecake is the perfect breakfast and chocolate is a food group all on its own.

~When my husband, Jim, and I moved to London, I entered the Cordon Bleu Cooking School. Living in and traveling through Europe, however, taught me more than I could ever learn in class. In school I was taught proper cooking techniques, but the vast array of new and wonderful ingredients I had never tasted at home, available to me in London and in my travels, had a far greater impact on my cooking—and eating. The Italian owners of the little *salumeria* around the corner from our flat in St. John's Wood introduced me to fresh, sweet *mascarpone* cheese and the now-popular *tiramisu*. This dessert, with its layers of spongy *génoise* soaked in espresso syrup and layered with *mascarpone* and rum zabaglione and covered with grated sweet chocolate, was incredible. I carried large chunks of it home and Jim and I ate it out of the same bowl with a spoon.

~On the rare, hot days that first summer in London, we threw open the windows and sat near the breezy openings eating big bowls of fresh English raspberries covered in double cream. England is a wonderland of fabulous dairy products, and no American ever forgets the first time they tasted this luxurious cream. The double cream came in small one-cup plastic containers covered with tin foil. I divided one of these cups between the two of us for a simple supper of fruit and cream. Sometimes I would scoop the fleshy, aromatic seeds from knobby shells of passion fruit and stir them into the cream. The combination of the perfumed passion fruit, thick cream, and tart berries is a taste sensation I will always remember.

~I brought these wonderful food memories—and an additional twenty pounds—home with me. When I started working as the pastry chef at the Golden Door, one of America's oldest and most renowned fitness spas, I wondered if I could create delicious sweets without the ever-present dessert-recipe trio of butter, cream, and eggs. Could I create desserts similar to the ones I loved but without the fat and calories? I wanted to devise guilt-free indulgences, artfully prepared and bursting with the richness and flavor that only the finest ingredients can impart.

~I started by researching the many diet dessert books on the market, but I was soon discouraged. Many of the health-conscious recipes, with their reliance on wheat germ, peanut butter, and sunflower seeds, were just too earthy-crunchy for me. Plus, those ingredients tend to make recipes very high in fat. Besides, I wasn't searching for desserts that delivered an entire day's worth of fiber and vitamins. I just wanted to eliminate my new enemy—fat—while still emphasizing good flavor and a pleasurable experience. After all, dessert is the part of the meal that should surprise and delight. Other diet dessert books I scoured were full of recipes concocted primarily of artificial sweeteners, egg substitutes, and food coloring. The dishes were insubstantial, artificial, and screamed "diet" with the very first bite.

~So, without a proper guidebook to follow, I started my quest for guilt-free desserts. I began examining the dessert recipes I loved baking and eating while in Europe, as well as the more familiar American desserts I had enjoyed while growing up. Could they be transformed into low-fat versions? Scrutinizing the fat content in each recipe and deciphering exactly what these fats did, I tried to create natural fat substitutes that achieved the same, or nearly the same, effect. Through trial and error I experimented to perfect fat substitutes. Then I created new recipes and revised traditional favorites that every fat and calorie counter could enjoy with an easy conscience.

~In a society that supports the ethic of eating to live not living to eat, those of us who still enjoy the rich tapestry of taste and experience that preparing and eating desserts provides need to find some balance that will maintain our health, our figures, and our well-being. This is a book for the thoughtful gourmand, for the dessert lover who wants to satisfy that craving for sweets every day without advertising the fact by the fit of his or her jeans. Although the desserts I have fashioned in this book are moderately sweet and very low in fat, they still capture the essence of what a good dessert is all about—pure pleasure.

~The desserts that follow cover a wide spectrum of tastes suitable for every occasion, from family suppers to elegant dinner parties. Some are quick and easy; others are more elaborate creations that require advance planning. With desserts ranging from raspberry sorbet and oatmeal-chocolate chip cookies to apricot cobbler and chocolate torte, there is a dessert for every whim. And with all of the recipes well under 180 calories and 30 percent fat per serving, they can be indulged in with abandon by everyone keeping a close eye on fat and calorie consumption.

The Basics

*a*re you sure this isn't fattening?" was something both the staff and the guests often asked me while I was the pastry chef at the Golden Door Fitness Spa. There is no better compliment to someone who has created a low-fat dessert than to be questioned about how fattening it really is! Creating desserts rich in taste, texture, and variety is not an easy feat, but by learning a few helpful techniques you can not only prepare the desserts in this volume, but also learn how to reduce the fat in your own favorite dessert recipes.

~For many years, the American Heart Association has attempted to wake up Americans to their excessive daily fat consumption, which for many people escalates to over 50 percent of their daily calorie intake. They have developed guidelines that specify the amount of fat and calories one should consume each day, for people either trying to lose weight or maintain their weight. The Heart Association recommends that Americans reduce their fat intake to no more than 30 percent of their daily calorie intake. The chart (right) is an example of how many calories and how much fat an individual should consume on both reducing and maintenance diets:

MAINTENANCE DIET (30 PERCENT FAT)	
MALE	FEMALE
2400 calories	1600 calories
80 grams of fat	53 grams of fat

REDUCING DIET (30 PERCENT FAT)	
MALE	FEMALE
1600 calories	1200 calories
53 grams of fat	40 grams of fat

~Sheri Shansby Boyden, a registered dietician with the Mayo Clinic in Rochester, Minnesota, devised an easy tool for fat watchers. The nutritional data on packaged foods lists the calories and, usually, the grams of fat per serving. To figure out the percentage of fat in each serving, Boyden uses an easy system she calls Fat Math. First, multiply the total grams of fat per serving by 9 (the amount of calories in 1 gram fat). Then divide this number of fat calories by the total calories per serving. Finally, multiply this number by 100 to determine the percentage of fat.

For example:
Italian Ricotta Cheesecake
124 calories and 2.2 grams of fat per serving.
$2.2 \times 9 = 19.8$ fat calories per serving.
19.8 divided by 124 (calories per serving)
$= .1596 \times 100 = 15.96$ or *16 percent* of calories from fat per serving.

~But what does this mean when we start talking about real food? Most people have a good idea of how much they can eat on a 1,200 calorie diet, but how much fat is 40 grams? What can one "buy" with a daily bank account of 40 grams? In the dessert world, not much. A small slice of apple pie is 420 calories and 16 grams fat, an average slice of chocolate cake is 630 calories and 25 grams fat, a sliver of New York cheesecake weighs in with a whopping 670 calories and 49 grams fat, and last but not least, *creme brulée* tops the charts with 588 calories and 50 grams fat per serving. When a small or average-sized dessert depletes the daily bank account of allowable fat, it is time to find an alternative to satisfying that sweet tooth. Every recipe in this volume includes the amount of calories, the grams of fat, and the percentage of fat per serving. This information is invaluable when attempting to calculate your daily diet, and will allow you to decide just how many calories and grams of fat you wish to "spend" on dessert.

~The challenge in creating low-fat, low-calorie desserts lies in producing something that not only tastes wonderful, but is beautiful as well. The best desserts delight the eye as well as the palate; presentation and taste are equally important in the creation of an outstanding dessert. Low-fat desserts, if successful, should closely resemble their more caloric counterparts, emphasizing the flavor of that dessert rather than the richness that butter, cream, and other fat-laden ingredients would impart. In order to create such desserts, it is necessary to find substitutes for high-fat ingredients that will not sacrifice the texture and flavor of the original dessert.

The Purpose of Fat in Baking

~Fats, especially butter, shortening, oils, and cream, play an important technical role in the successful execution of many desserts. In layer cakes, pound cakes, sweet breads, and muffins, fats aid in developing the flours and regulating the consistency and tenderness of a batter. When butter or shortening and sugar are creamed together, the sugar crystals react with the fat to create air pockets that are then incorporated into the batter. These air pockets make a more tender cake with an even, nongrainy texture, and they aerate the mixture to give it leavening power (usually assisted by the addition of eggs and/or baking powder and baking soda). If all or part of the butter or shortening is eliminated, these vital functions need to be performed by another method. For example, whipping the sugar with the eggs instead of butter will create the air pockets that aid in leavening. Adding the eggs at this stage helps eliminate part of the high-fat content of the dessert.

~Fats have more to do than just assist in leavening, however. They also contribute moisture and a richer "mouth appeal" to the finished product. What would a pound cake be, after, all, without its pound of butter? To maintain the luxurious flavor butter, oils, and shortening contribute, other ingredients must be used as moistening agents. Fruit butters and fruit and vegetable purées are high in moisture and can give added flavor and richness to many baked goods. Bananas are a popular choice, but pumpkin or sweet potato purée, apple and pear butters, and puréed cooked carrots are all possibilities. When eliminating fat from a recipe, it is important to substitute an equal weight of a fat substitute to maintain the structural integrity of the dessert and to ensure a successful finished product. In other words, if you are using banana purée as a substitute for part of the butter in a given recipe, use the same amount of banana as you would butter. For example, a mixture of 4 ounces butter and 4 ounces banana purée will be a successful substitute for 8 ounces butter.

~Another technique deals not with fats and their substitutes, but with the sugars and other sweeteners used in a particular recipe. Sugar not only adds sweetness to a dessert, it also plays a structural role with fats in tenderizing and preserving the finished dessert. If fats are limited or eliminated completely, sugar alone cannot maintain the tenderness and moistness of the final dessert. Liquid sweeteners like honey, maple syrup, molasses, and corn syrup have qualities, along with sweetening power, that granulated sugar alone lacks. Thick and rich and highly flavored, these sweeteners can add a complex flavor and create the same moist nature that the butter-sugar combination imparts. Acting as humectants, liquid sweeteners not only stop the process of moisture loss in baked goods, they actually draw moisture from the environment to keep cakes, muffins, and sweet breads moist and tasty. The standard rule for substituting liquid sweeteners for granulated sugar is ¾ cup liquid sweetener per 1 cup granulated sugar. The cook would also decrease the amount of liquid in the recipe by ¼ cup.

~Since the idea is not only to use a substitute sweetener, but also to reduce fat, use a fruit or vegetable purée for part of the fat or oil in the recipe. The humectant qualities of the fruit purée when combined with the liquid sweetener will deliver a satisfyingly moist product. A good example of this method is pumpkin gingerbread on page 52. Although the cook would normally decrease the liquids by ¼ cup in such cases, a little experimentation is necessary when attempting to reduce the fat in traditional recipes. Creating low-fat dessert recipes isn't an exact science, so trial and error is part of the process.

~It is important to analyze all the functions fats perform in a dessert in order to choose the best fat substitute for the job. Structure, moistness, richness, and flavor all require either a change in technique when making the recipe or a suitable flavor-enhancing fat substitute to succeed. For example, a traditional fruit mousse relies on whipped cream to enhance and enrich the fruit flavor used and to give a smooth creamy finish and some body and structure to the dessert. A good substitute for the cream is the fromage frais on page 23, a soft, mild cheese made from equal portions of nonfat plain yogurt and cottage cheese puréed together until smooth and then strained of any liquid. This substitute will give the new fat-free dessert the creamy finish of whipped cream but not the same light, firm body and structure needed for a mousse. But if you add Swiss meringue and set the mixture lightly with gelatin, this revised mousse will have a taste and texture similar to its high-fat counterpart. For a Swiss meringue, egg whites and sugar are warmed together before whipping, giving the meringue better volume and stability and a firmer texture.

Using Fat Substitutes

~Since many fats are dairy based, I began experimenting with fat substitutes made from low-fat or nonfat dairy products. Using classic pastry- and dessert-making techniques but different ingredients, I was able to reduce dramatically the amount of fat and still create a successful, good-tasting dessert. Some experiments, however, were more successful than others. I discovered that completely butter-free pastry crust is bland and doughy. But if I substituted half the required butter in the original recipe with low-fat cottage cheese and reduced the water, the result was a tender, flavorful crust with half the fat. Nonfat plain yogurt is a great substitute for sour cream in many recipes, and when it is fully drained to form a soft, fresh cheese, it can substitute for crème fraîche or cream cheese. Low-fat ricotta cheese and cottage cheese, skim milk, and buttermilk can all substitute for higher-fat products when treated correctly.

~Following is a list of high-fat items and the low-fat substitutes that can replace them:

Butter
Vegetable oil, low-calorie margarine, fruit and vegetable purées, fruit butters.

~These substitutes work best when the butter is used as a moistening and enriching agent. If butter is being creamed with sugar to help aerate a cake, for example, oil or fruit purées are poor stand-ins and more complicated methods are needed to aerate the batter. Begin by replacing half the butter in a recipe with one of these substitutes to see how successful the result is. Canola oil, made from rape seed, is very low in saturated fats and very mild in flavor, and is therefore a good all-around oil for using in low-fat recipes.

Sour Cream
Nonfat plain yogurt, yogurt cheese (page 23).

~Substitute equal portions of these ingredients for sour cream.

Cream
Buttermilk, yogurt cheese (page 23), fromage frais (page 23), pot cheese (page 22), ricotta cheese.

~Where the cream remains liquid, buttermilk can be substituted. Yogurt cheese or pot cheese can act as a partial substitute for whipped cream. The addition of beaten egg white and a little gelatin will help round out the effect, especially in mousses, Bavarians, and cake fillings.

Cream Cheese
Yogurt cheese (page 23), fromage frais (page 23), pot cheese (page 22), ricotta cheese.

~Some people find yogurt cheese to be too tart, so a combination of yogurt cheese and pot cheese, fromage frais, or ricotta cheese can be used.

Whole Milk
Nonfat milk, low-fat milk, buttermilk, nonfat condensed milk, low-fat condensed milk.

Flavor Layering

~Since fats intensify and enrich the flavors of other foods, it is important to develop a new way to enhance flavors that eliminates the fat but allows the full essence of the ingredients to shine through. The diner's palate must never miss the creamy finish of fat.

~To solve this problem, I originated a technique I have christened "flavor layering." For example, if I am creating an orange-flavored dessert I try to use as many high-quality, natural orange-flavored ingredients as possible to create the most complex and intense flavor experience. Fresh, ripe oranges and freshly squeezed orange juice coupled with an orange liqueur such as Grand Marnier or Curaçao and a pure orange extract may all be used in the same dessert. The palate is stimulated and interested and the fat is not missed.

~Since flavor layering emphasizes flavor and not fat, it is important to use the highest-quality ingredients available. Using only the finest liqueurs, fruits and natural—never artificial—flavoring agents and extracts is very important. Purchase vanilla beans and pure vanilla and fruit extracts. Team the finest fruit brandies such as Calvados and poire Williams with the ripest, freshest apples and pears available. Combine coffee liqueurs with superior cocoa powder—both regular and Dutch-process—for intensely chocolatey, never bitter desserts. Natural chocolate extract is available and, along with the flavor of coffee, enhances and enriches the taste of chocolate. Dark Jamaican rum highlights the sweetness in a honey-laced yogurt sauce, and orange-scented Essencia wine and fresh mint accent a variety of ripe summer melons. Adding only the best ingredients is critical because there is no butter or cream to mask the taste of an underripe fruit or the aftertaste of an inferior vanilla extract.

~One trick I developed that shows off the advantages of flavor layering gives low-fat or nonfat frozen yogurt and ice milk a needed flavor lift. Since they contain so little fat, these frozen desserts can have an unappealing icy texture. Infused with inexpensive or imitation flavorings, they can come across at best as bland, and at worst artificial. But if you flavor plain vanilla frozen yogurt or ice milk yourself, such as in the recipes for cappuccino fudge roulade on page 86, and the raspberry-lemon parfait on page 99, the finished product will be memorable. Vanilla ice milk flavor layered with fresh lemon juice, chopped lemon zest, and a touch of pure lemon extract becomes a frozen dessert that virtually explodes with flavor. Whipping together the frozen yogurt or ice milk and these flavoring agents using a mixer aerates the icy texture of the fat-free dessert, breaking down the larger ice crystals and creating an ice milk or frozen yogurt similar in texture to premium high-fat ice creams. Lemon is one flavoring, but orange, lime, tropical-fruit purées, berries, coffee, and liqueurs all make successful flavoring agents with this technique.

The Roles of Eggs and Sugar

~Eggs and sugar play critical roles not only in the taste, but also in the structure of desserts. Both are necessary components in good baking. Sugar acts as a sweetener and a tenderizer. Eggs moisten dry ingredients, assist in aerating the batter to create a lighter, more tender product, and, combined with flour, form a stabilized structure for cakes, muffins, or sweet breads. Although sugar is calorically dense and eggs contain fat and cholesterol, instead of eliminating them and thus eliminating the vital roles they play, I have reduced the quantity.

~One method some cooks employ to reduce the calories and fat in eggs is to use egg whites alone. Unfortunately, this can lead to a rubbery texture. A better solution is to reduce the amount of yolks, but not eliminate them completely, and add additional egg whites for the yolks that have been eliminated. A simple formula is to substitute 1 whole egg and 2 egg whites for every 2 whole eggs. I prefer to avoid commercial egg substitutes and artificial sweeteners and to rely instead on natural substitutes.

Ingredients and Equipment

~Two ingredients and a few kitchen tools are indispensable to the cook interested in making low-fat desserts on a regular basis. The first ingredient is vegetable coating spray (PAM is a popular brand), which is made from lecithin and oil. Commonly available in aerosol cans, this product is available in environmentally sound nonaerosol pump bottles as well. It comes in unflavored, butter-flavored, and even olive oil-flavored varieties and is invaluable for greasing cake pans and Bavarian molds. It is also a handy, low-fat way to lubricate the layers of phyllo dough that comprise many of the pastries in this book.

~The second important ingredient is phyllo dough. It is wonderful for making crisp pastry shells, napoleon layers, and strudels of all flavors. Although it is not difficult to work with, it can be intimidating for the first time user. Carefully follow the instructions on the box if you are purchasing frozen phyllo dough. It is important to thaw the dough in the refrigerator for 12 to 24 hours, or the pastry sheets will stick together when they are unfolded. Phyllo sheets have a low moisture content, so once they have been removed from the refrigerator and unwrapped, they should be covered with a cool, damp cloth to prevent them from drying out. It also helps to work quickly and without interruptions.

~Parchment paper, a nonstick baking paper stocked in most kitchenware shops and some larger grocery stores, is used to line pans to prevent cakes and pastries that contain little or no fat from sticking as they bake. If you cannot find parchment paper, waxed paper can be used to line cake pans and aluminum foil can be used on baking sheets. Parchment paper does a superior job, however.

~Although a hand-held electric mixer will suffice for most of the tasks in this book and is even necessary for some of the recipes with small amounts of eggs or liquids, a large free-standing heavy-duty mixer such as a Kitchen Aid is a wonderful tool. It is ideal for recipes in which many eggs must be warmed and then whipped to a great volume, such as the butter-free *génoise* on page 26 or a Swiss meringue.

~For smaller tasks such as incorporating ingredients or folding meringue mixtures into cakes, mousses or Bavarians, a large metal balloon whisk and large rubber spatula are ideal. Most cooks will already have these tools in their kitchen; if you do not, they are easily purchased at any kitchenware shop. A roulade, or jelly-roll pan, madeleine tins, dariole molds, and cream horn molds are called for in these pages. If you do not already own these specialized items, they are not too expensive and can be used to make many other desserts.

~Finally, one of the most unusual tools I recommend for the home cook is the blow torch. Small household torches available in most hardware stores for under $25 are commonly found in restaurant kitchens. They run on propane and are not powerful enough to do any major welding. The torch is used to caramelize sugar topping. It hardens the sugar without heating the dessert beneath it the way a hot broiler usually does. If a torch is unavailable, or if you feel uncomfortable working with it, use a hot broiler, watching carefully so the dessert does not burn.

~The recipes that follow include detailed instructions for making the various fat substitutes plus recipes for chocolate, fruit, and creamy sauces designed to en-hance the flavor and presentation of your new low-fat, low-calorie desserts. These desserts do not have to replace completely your favorite sweet finales. The occasional substitute of a low-fat dessert for a higher-fat one gives you the enjoyment and pleasure that making and eating desserts provide without adding too much fat to your daily diet. This allows you to splurge on that ultrarich crème brulée and not have to go without for the rest of the week.

Vanilla Sugar

~This delicately scented sugar, used in place of plain granulated sugar, adds a subtle, complex flavor to desserts. It will keep indefinitely and can be replenished by adding more granulated sugar to the container after portions of the flavored sugar have been used. Look for moist, plump vanilla beans to deliver the most intense flavor.

Makes 3 cups

3 cups granulated sugar
1 vanilla bean

~Place the sugar in a jar with a tight-fitting lid. Split the vanilla bean in half lengthwise. Using the tip of a sharp paring knife, scrape the seeds from the pod into the sugar. Stir to distribute the seeds throughout the sugar. Then add the pods to the sugar. To strengthen the flavors, cover tightly and store in a cool, dry place for at least 1 week before using.

~To replenish the vanilla sugar, simply replace the vanilla sugar used with an equal amount of plain granulated sugar. After 1 or 2 months, the vanilla bean may lose its scent and will need to be replaced with a fresh vanilla bean. The amount of time depends upon the freshness of the original vanilla bean.

Per tablespoon: 45 calories
0 grams fat ~ 0% calories from fat

Lemon sugar: Omit the vanilla bean. Add the pared zest, without any white pith, of 2 fresh lemons to the sugar.

Orange or tangerine sugar: Omit the vanilla bean. Add the pared zest, without any white pith, of 2 fresh oranges or tangerines to the sugar.

Vanilla Sugar Syrup

~Here is a light sugar syrup that is a wonderful, fat-free way to sweeten and intensify the flavors of fruit butters, sauces, and poached fruit. Use it as a base for cocoa fudge sauce (page 25) or to sweeten fruit compotes.

Makes about 1½ cups

1 vanilla bean
1 cup water
1 cup granulated sugar

~Split the vanilla bean in half lengthwise. Combine the water and sugar in a 1-quart saucepan over medium heat and stir to dissolve the sugar. When the sugar dissolves, using the tip of a sharp paring knife, scrape the seeds from the pod into the pan, then add the pod to the pan as well. Increase the heat to high and bring the syrup to a boil. Boil for 1 minute. Remove from the heat and let cool completely. Refrigerate the syrup in a tightly covered container. It will keep for about 1 month.

Per tablespoon: 30 calories
0 grams fat ~ 0% calories from fat

Plain sugar syrup: Omit the vanilla bean. Proceed as for vanilla syrup.

Lemon sugar syrup: Omit the vanilla bean. Use ½ cup freshly squeezed lemon juice in place of ½ cup of the water. Add the pared zest, without any white pith, of 1 lemon once the sugar dissolves. Proceed as for vanilla syrup.

Orange sugar syrup: Omit vanilla bean. Add 2 tablespoons orange juice concentrate and the pared zest, without any white pith, of 1 orange once the sugar dissolves. Proceed as for vanilla syrup.

Coffee sugar syrup: Substitute 1 cup brewed coffee for the water. Proceed as for vanilla syrup.

Liqueur sugar syrup: Omit the vanilla bean. When the syrup is cool, stir in 2 tablespoons liqueur of choice: Grand Marnier, Kahlúa, dark Jamaican rum, Framboise, crème de menthe and Frangelico are good choices.

Honey-Yogurt Sauce

~This quick sauce can dress up fresh fruit, or it can be squeezed from a squirt bottle to make designs on a fruit coulis for an extravagant dessert presentation. Use a fragrant honey; lavender or blackberry is a good choice. For a creamier sauce, see vanilla bean crème anglaise on page 25.

Makes about 2 cups

2 cups nonfat plain yogurt
2 tablespoons honey
2 teaspoons pure vanilla extract
½ vanilla bean

~In a small bowl whisk together the yogurt, honey, and vanilla extract. Split the vanilla bean in half lengthwise and, using the tip of a sharp paring knife, scrape the seeds into the yogurt. Whisk the yogurt to distribute the seeds. (Do not discard the pod; add it to granulated sugar to make the vanilla sugar on page 21.) Cover and refrigerate for at least 1 hour to allow the flavors to blend. The sauce will keep for about 1 week, in the refrigerator.

Per tablespoon: 12 calories
0 grams fat ~ 0% calories from fat

Pot Cheese

~This lightly sweetened, creamy cheese is a perfect filling for blintzes or crepes, and is a good base for cheesecakes.

Makes about 1¼ cups

2 cups low-fat (1%) cottage cheese
1 tablespoon granulated sugar
1 teaspoon pure vanilla extract

~In a food processor fitted with a metal blade or in a blender, combine the cottage cheese and sugar and purée until creamy, thick, and smooth. Stir in the vanilla. Pour the mixture into a large sieve lined with a double thickness of cheesecloth, and place the sieve over a large bowl to catch the liquid. Refrigerate for 24 hours.

~When the cheese is ready, discard the liquid. Store the cheese in a tightly covered container in the refrigerator for up to 1 week.

Per tablespoon: 16 calories
0.2 grams fat ~ 11% calories from fat

Yogurt Cheese

~Yogurt strained of its liquids yields a soft, tart cheese with a consistency similar to cream cheese. The addition of nonfat milk powder tempers the acidity of nonfat yogurt without adding additional fat calories. Remember to buy yogurt that contains no carageenan, gelatin, cornstarch, or other thickeners; they prevent the yogurt from releasing its whey so that it can form the cheese. This is a good, if slightly tart, substitute for cream cheese and an important component of low-fat cheesecakes.

Makes about 2 cups

4 cups nonfat plain yogurt
¼ cup nonfat milk powder (optional)

~In a bowl stir together the yogurt and the milk powder, if using. Pour the yogurt mixture into a large metal sieve lined with a double thickness of cheesecloth and place the sieve over a large bowl to catch the liquid. Refrigerate for 24 hours.

When the cheese is ready, it will be like a soft cream cheese. Discard the liquid. Store the cheese in a tightly covered container in the refrigerator for up to 1 week.

Per tablespoon: 18 calories
0 grams fat ~ 0% calories from fat

Fromage Frais

~Less tangy and slightly softer than yogurt cheese (this page), this cheese is a good substitute for whipped cream in mousses, chilled soufflés, and Bavarians.

Makes about 2¼ cups

2 cups low-fat (1%) cottage cheese
2 cups nonfat plain yogurt

~In a food processor fitted with a metal blade or in a blender, purée the cottage cheese until it is creamy, thick, and smooth. Turn the purée out into a bowl and fold the yogurt into it. Pour the mixture into a large sieve lined with a double thickness of cheesecloth and place the sieve over a large bowl to catch the liquid. Refrigerate for 24 hours.

~When the cheese is ready, discard the liquid. Store the cheese in a tightly covered container in the refrigerator for up to 1 week.

Per tablespoon: 16 calories
0.2 grams fat ~ 11% calories from fat

Pear Butter

~Similar to apple butter (page 24), but smoother and mellower. Cardamom gives this fruit butter a heavenly sweet perfume that makes it a particularly tasty base for a light pear soufflé.

Makes about 1¼ cups

4 Bosc or Anjou pears (1¾ to 2 pounds), peeled, cored, and chopped
3 tablespoons vanilla sugar syrup (page 21)
½ teaspoon ground cinnamon
½ teaspoon ground cardamom
pinch of ground cloves

~Combine the pears, syrup, and spices in a 2-quart saucepan over high heat. Cover and bring to a boil. Reduce the heat to medium-low and simmer, stirring occasionally, until the pears are soft and translucent, 20 to 30 minutes. If the liquid evaporates before the pears are cooked, add ¼ cup water and continue cooking. Transfer the pear mixture to a food processor fitted with a metal blade or to a blender and process to form a smooth purée. Alternatively, pass the mixture through a food mill.

~Return the purée to the saucepan. Cook over medium heat, stirring constantly, for about 10 minutes, to reduce further the liquid content of the pear mixture. The pear butter should have the consistency of thick honey. Store in a covered container in the refrigerator for up to 2 weeks.

Per tablespoon: 25 calories
0 grams fat ~ 0% calories from fat

Apple Butter

~Spicy, tart, and sweet all in the same mouthful. This concentrated fruit spread is easy to make and very versatile. Substitute apple butter for a portion of the butter or oil used in quick breads, layer it beneath apples in a warm fruit tart, or simply slather it on a slice of toasted bread.

Makes about 1 cup

4 medium Golden Delicious apples (about 1¾ pounds total weight), peeled, cored, and chopped
¼ cup vanilla sugar syrup (page 21)
¼ teaspoon ground ginger
¼ teaspoon ground cinnamon
¼ teaspoon fresh ground nutmeg

~Combine the apples, syrup, and spices in a 2-quart saucepan over high heat. Cover and bring to a boil. Reduce the heat to medium-low and simmer, stirring occasionally, until the apples are soft and translucent, 20 to 30 minutes. If the liquid evaporates before the apples are cooked, *add ½ cup water and continue cooking.* Transfer the apple mixture to a food processor fitted with a metal blade or to a blender and purée until smooth. Alternatively, pass the mixture through a food mill.

~Return the purée to the saucepan. Cook over medium heat, stirring constantly, for about 10 minutes, to reduce further the liquid content of the apple mixture. The butter should be a thick, cinnamon-colored spread with the consistency of thick honey. Store in a covered container in the refrigerator for up to 2 weeks.

Per tablespoon: 26 calories
0 grams fat ~ 0% calories from fat

Cranberry Coulis

~The beautiful ruby color and tart flavor of this fruit coulis goes particularly well with rich chocolate desserts. Serve a few spoonfuls of it with chocolate seashells (page 72) or chocolate génoise (page 75), or layer it with vanilla ice cream, ice milk, or frozen yogurt for a festive holiday parfait.

1 cup cranberries
2 cups apple juice
1 or 2 teaspoons granulated sugar (optional)

~Combine the cranberries and apple juice in a 1-quart saucepan and bring to a boil over high heat. Reduce the heat to low and simmer, stirring occasionally, until the cranberries are very soft, about 10 minutes.

~Transfer the cranberry mixture to a food processor fitted with a metal blade or to a blender and purée. Pass the purée through a fine-mesh sieve to remove any seeds or fibers, then sweeten it with 1 or 2 teaspoons sugar if it is too tart. Cover and refrigerate until ready to serve.

Per tablespoon: 7 calories
0 grams fat ~ 0% calories from fat

Fruit Coulis

~A coulis is a sauce made from puréed fruits or vegetables. These sauces are vibrant and fresh tasting and very easy to make. They are delicious with many of the desserts in this book, or as the flavoring base for mousses or soufflés. A coulis can be successfully frozen for up to 2 months.

Makes about 2 cups

1 pound fresh or frozen strawberries, blackberries, raspberries, kiwifruits, peaches, or nectarines, or 1½ pounds papayas or mangoes
1 tablespoon granulated sugar (optional)
2 tablespoons complementary liqueur (see note)
2 tablespoons freshly squeezed lemon juice, if using peaches or nectarines

~If using frozen fruit, thaw at room temperature. Peel and pit the fruit, if necessary, and place in a food processor fitted with a metal blade or in a blender. (If using the kiwifruits, use a food processor only. A blender breaks up the seeds and causes the sauce to be bitter and speckled with black flecks that cannot be sieved out.) Purée the fruit, then pass it through a fine-mesh sieve to remove any seeds.

~Sweeten the purée with sugar if it is too tart, and then stir in the liqueur. If using peach or nectarine purée, stir in the lemon juice to prevent the purée from discoloring.

Note: Suggested complementary liquor and fruit combinations include Midori with kiwifruit; Grand Marnier with strawberry, nectarine or raspberry; Framboise with raspberry; Chambord with blackberry; peach brandy or Amaretto with peach; Grand Passion or dark Jamaican rum with papaya or mango.

Per tablespoon: 9 calories
0 grams fat ~ 0% calories from fat

Vanilla Bean Crème Anglaise

~Dark, chocolate desserts are enhanced by this creamy vanilla custard sauce. For a very light simple dessert, serve fresh berries with this custard sauce and raspberry coulis (page 24).

Makes about 2 cups

1 cup nonfat milk
½ vanilla bean
¼ cup low-fat (1%) cottage cheese
1 egg
3 tablespoons vanilla sugar (page 21) or
*   plain granulated sugar*
1 teaspoon cornstarch
½ teaspoon pure vanilla extract

~Pour the milk into a small saucepan. Split the vanilla bean in half lengthwise and, using the tip of a sharp paring knife, scrape the seeds into the milk. Add the pods to the milk as well and heat over medium heat just until bubbles form at the edges of the pan. Remove from the heat, cover, and let stand for 5 minutes to allow the vanilla flavor to infuse the milk.

~Meanwhile, in a food processor fitted with a metal blade or in a blender, combine the cottage cheese, egg, sugar, and cornstarch. Process until smooth. Remove the vanilla pods from the milk and pour the milk over the cottage cheese mixture. Pulse once or twice in the food processor or blender to combine.

~Pour the mixture back into the saucepan and stir continuously over very gentle heat until the mixture thickens and coats the back of a spoon, 3 to 5 minutes. Do not overheat or the mixture may curdle. Remove from the heat and stir in the vanilla extract. Pour the sauce through a fine-mesh sieve into a 2-cup container, cover, and chill well before using. This sauce will keep covered in the refrigerator for up to 1 week.

Per tablespoon: 12 calories
0 grams fat ~ 0% calories from fat

Cocoa Fudge Sauce

~This flavorful, low-fat fudge sauce becomes darker, richer, and mellower when Dutch-process cocoa is used. Top slices of *génoise* or angel food cake with a scoop of frozen yogurt or ice milk and smother in fresh strawberries and this fudge sauce. Or substitute this sauce for the melted semisweet chocolate in some of your favorite fattening chocolate recipes. Remember, though, this sauce will not firm up as well as semisweet chocolate will.

Makes about 1½ cups

1 cup water
¾ cup granulated sugar
1 cup Dutch-process cocoa powder
1 teaspoon pure vanilla extract

~Combine the water and sugar in a 1-quart saucepan over medium heat and stir to dissolve the sugar. Increase the heat to high and bring the liquid to a rolling boil to form a sugar syrup. Let the syrup boil for about 1 minute. Remove from the heat and whisk in the cocoa powder. Return the pan to medium heat and whisk until the sauce is smooth and thick, 3 to 5 minutes. Remove from the heat and whisk in the vanilla extract.

Let the sauce cool completely; it will thicken slightly as it cools. Store the sauce in a tightly covered container for up to 1 month in the refrigerator.

Per tablespoon: 38 calories
.38 grams fat ~ 9% calories from fat

Double-vanilla fudge sauce: Substitute 1 cup vanilla sugar syrup (page 22) for the plain sugar syrup

Mocha fudge sauce: Substitute 1 cup brewed coffee for the water

Orange fudge sauce: Add 1 teaspoon freshly grated orange zest with the cocoa to the sugar syrup and stir 1 tablespoon Grand Marnier into the finished sauce.

Butter-Free Génoise

~The "warm-method" is used for making this delicate cake. Eggs and sugar are warmed in a mixing bowl over low heat before whipping. Heating dissolves the sugar crystals and prevents them from re-granulating after baking and cooling, which is what coarsens a cake's texture. The result is a fine-textured sponge cake that stays moist longer. There is no butter in this *génoise*, which not only reduces the calories and fat content but also the shelf life. The absence of butter does not harm the cake's texture or taste, however. Simply serve it the day it is baked, or wrap it well and freeze for up to 1 month. Variations on this *génoise*, appear in the recipes for strawberry Bavarian cake (page 48), lemon-poppy seed strawberry shortcake (page 60), fresh pineapple upside-down cake (page 56), and apricot cobbler (page 63).

~This is a good basic cake that is handy to have stored in the freezer for last-minute desserts. Top slices with vanilla frozen yogurt, fresh fruit, and complementary fruit coulis (page 24) or cocoa fudge sauce (page 25). Bake the batter in a roulade pan and fill the cake with the lemon-flavored frozen yogurt used in raspberry-lemon parfait (page 99) or another flavor that you have concocted on your own, or make a fruit shortcake with fresh fruit and frozen yogurt or sweetened yogurt cheese (page 23).

Makes three 8-inch cake layers, two 9-by-13-inch roulades, or 2 dozen cupcakes

8 eggs
1 cup vanilla or lemon sugar (page 21)
  or plain granulated sugar
½ teaspoon freshly grated lemon zest
¼ teaspoon ground cardamom
¼ teaspoon freshly grated nutmeg
1 teaspoon pure vanilla extract
2 cups cake flour, sifted twice
pinch of salt

~Preheat an oven to 350° F. Line three 8-inch round cake pans or two 9-by-13-inch roulade pans with parchment paper and then spray them with a vegetable coating spray. If you are making cupcakes, simply spray the cupcake tins with the vegetable coating spray.

~Combine the eggs, sugar, lemon zest, and spices in a metal or other heatproof bowl. Place the bowl in a large sauté pan filled halfway with simmering water and whisk continuously until the sugar crystals dissolve and the mixture is hot to the touch (120° F), about 3 to 4 minutes. Remove the bowl from the water and beat the egg mixture with the whisk attachment of a mixer set on high speed until the batter triples in volume and the bowl is cool to the touch, about 5 minutes. Beat in the vanilla extract.

~Sift the flour a third time, this time with the salt. Using a balloon whisk or a large rubber spatula, gently fold the flour, one third at a time, into the batter.

~Spoon the batter into the chosen pans and bake in the preheated oven until puffed and golden and the top springs back to the touch, 12 to 15 minutes (cupcakes may take less time). Remove from the oven and let cool on a wire rack for 5 minutes. Run a thin metal spatula around the edge of the pans and invert the cakes, roulades or cupcakes onto the rack. Peel off the parchment paper, if using. Cool completely before serving, or before wrapping and freezing. Each cake will yield 8 servings and each roulade will yield 12 servings.

Per cake slice or cupcake: 85 calories
2 grams fat ~ 21% calories from fat

Flaky Pastry

~Here is an all-purpose dough for pies, tarts, turnovers, or any recipe requiring a pastry crust. Unfortunately, it is nearly impossible to create a *good* pastry dough without butter, margarine, or shortening. Although this recipe has a relatively small amount of fat, the pastry is quite tender. It is easy to roll out and can take a lot of handling before becoming tough. Fill fully baked tartlet shells (see directions below) with sweetened yogurt cheese (page 23) or fromage frais (page 23) and top with fresh berries, nectarine or peach slices, or thin slivers of pineapple and kiwifruit. Or use this dough as a base for your favorite pie filling.

Makes one 9-inch pie shell or 8 tartlet shells

¾ cup all-purpose flour
¼ teaspoon salt
3 tablespoons unsalted butter, low-calorie
   stick margarine, or shortening, chilled
¼ cup low-fat (1%) cottage cheese
2 or 3 tablespoons ice water

~Sift together the flour and salt 3 times. Place the sifted mixture in the work bowl of a food processor fitted with a metal blade. Cut the chilled butter, margarine, or shortening into small bits and add with the cottage cheese to the processor. Process, using brief on-off pulses, until the mixture is crumbly. Do not overprocess. Add the ice water, 1 tablespoon at a time, and process again using brief on-off pulses just until the dough comes together. Remove the dough from the processor and pat it

into a small disk. Wrap the disk in plastic wrap and refrigerate for 30 minutes before rolling out. Use the dough as directed in individual recipes.

~If you are making the dough by hand, in a bowl cut the chilled butter, margarine, or shortening into the sifted flour mixture with a pastry blender or 2 knives until crumbly. Dribble the ice water into the mixture, 1 tablespoon at a time, and, using your hands, mix lightly just until the dough comes together. Knead the dough gently, pat into a small disk and refrigerate for 30 minutes.

~For fully baked tartlet shells, preheat the oven to 350° F. Divide the dough into 8 equal portions. Spray 8 small tartlet tins lightly with vegetable coating spray. Using your thumbs, evenly press 1 portion of the chilled dough into each tin. Place the tartlet tins on a baking sheet. Line each tartlet with a small piece of parchment paper or aluminum foil and fill with raw beans or rice. Bake the tartlet shells in the preheated oven for 10 minutes. Remove from the oven and carefully remove the beans or rice by lifting out the parchment or foil liners. Save the beans or rice for another use and discard the parchment or foil. Return the tartlet shells to the oven and continue baking until the shells are crisp and a light golden brown, 4 to 7 minutes. Remove from the oven and cool completely before removing from the tins.

Per serving: 80 calories
4.4 grams fat ~ 49% calories from fat

Crêpes

~A good all-purpose crêpe that freezes well for future use.

Makes about 16 crêpes

2 eggs
1 cup nonfat milk
1 teaspoon canola oil
¼ teaspoon ground cinnamon
1 teaspoon granulated sugar
½ cup all-purpose flour
pinch of salt

~In a blender or a food processor fitted with a metal blade, combine all the ingredients and process for 1 minute until smooth. Cover and refrigerate at least 1 hour before making crêpes.

~Heat a 6-inch crêpe pan over medium heat and spray lightly with a vegetable coating spray. Ladle 2 tablespoons of the batter into the pan and tilt the pan to cover the bottom with a thin, even coating. Cook the crêpe until small bubbles form on the surface and it is barely firm, 30 seconds to 1 minute. Cook the crêpe on one side only and carefully remove from the pan by releasing the edges with a thin metal spatula and sliding it out onto a flat surface. Repeat with the remaining crêpe batter.

~Use crêpes immediately, or stack them, separated by waxed paper, wrap well, and freeze for up to 1 month. Thaw, while still wrapped, at room temperature.

Per crêpe: 30 calories
1 gram fat ~ 30% calories from fat

Elegant Finales

*P*astry chefs often produce whimsical, elaborate concoctions—delicate cakes artfully decorated with swirls of whipped cream and ruffles of chocolate, or fresh fruit and crisp pastry accented with a colorful fruit coulis or a rich, creamy sauce. Desserts are the most visually stunning creations of the culinary arts.

~Creating low-fat desserts that honor the pastry chef's art is especially difficult. A good dessert must intoxicate all the senses; it must satisfy the eye as well as the palate with clear, intense flavors, delicate textures, and delicious aromas. This is sometimes hard without the fattening crutches of butter and cream, but it is definitely not impossible.

~While it has become easier for the sophisticated host to whip up imaginative and delicious low-fat, low-calorie main-course fare, the search for an equally elegant finale worthy of the best pastry chef remains illusive. The following desserts satisfy these demands by combining creative presentation techniques with unique flavor combinations. Many of these desserts are comprised of two or more components that can be made in advance and assembled right before serving, making them perfect for entertaining. Desserts with such style and panache deserve an audience to dazzle!

Honey-Cornmeal Crêpes with Loganberries and Fromage Frais

~The coarse, grainy texture of these pale gold crêpes contrasts nicely with the tart, smooth fromage frais and ripe berries. Blackberries can be substituted for the loganberries.

Makes 12 servings

For the crêpes:
½ cup all-purpose flour
3 tablespoons yellow cornmeal
pinch of salt
1 whole egg plus 2 egg whites
½ cup nonfat milk
½ cup buttermilk
½ teaspoon baking soda
1 tablespoon honey
pinch of ground nutmeg
2 teaspoons canola oil

For the filling:
1½ cups fromage frais (page 23)
½ cup confectioners' sugar, sifted
3 cups loganberries or blackberries
2 to 3 tablespoons blackberry- or loganberry-flavored liqueur (optional)
confectioners' sugar for garnish (optional)

~In a blender or a food processor fitted with a metal blade, combine all the ingredients for the crêpes and blend until smooth, about 1 minute. Cover and refrigerate for 1 hour before cooking the crêpes.

~Heat a 6-inch crêpe pan until hot. Spray lightly with a vegetable coating spray. Stir the crêpe batter to make sure the cornmeal has not settled to the bottom. Ladle 1 tablespoon of the crêpe batter into the pan and tilt the pan to form a 3- to 4-inch crêpe. (To make forming the crêpe easier, place a 3- or 4-inch open-topped round biscuit or cookie cutter in the pan and pour in the batter so that it is trapped within the cutter). Cook the crêpe until small bubbles form on the surface and it is barely firm, about 1 minute. Remove the biscuit cutter, if using, and flip the crêpe over. Cook the second side for about 30 seconds, just enough time for it to firm up. Use a thin, metal spatula to slide the crêpe out onto a flat surface to cool. Repeat this process with the remaining crêpe batter, stirring the batter occasionally. There should be 24 to 26 crêpes.

~To fill the crêpes, combine the fromage frais and confectioners' sugar in a small bowl and stir until smooth. If desired, place the berries in another bowl, add the liqueur, and toss gently to mix well. Place 2 crêpes on each dessert plate. Spoon the fromage frais mixture into a pastry bag fitted with a medium-sized star tip and pipe about 1 tablespoon of the mixture down the center of each crêpe. Top each crêpe with about 2 tablespoons of the berries. Fold the crêpes over and sprinkle with additional confectioners' sugar, if desired.

Per serving: 125 calories
2 grams fat ~ 14% calories from fat

Phyllo Cornets with Raspberry-Rhubarb Mousse

~This is a beautiful dessert to present, perfect for the most elaborate dinner party. It may seem complicated, but the cornets, mousse, and berry coulis can all be prepared in advance and assembled just before serving. The result is a wonderful marriage of tastes and textures: crisp, sweet cornets combined with an intense, fruity mousse.

Makes 10 servings

For the phyllo cornets:
Butter-flavored vegetable coating spray
10 sheets phyllo dough (12 by 17 inches),
*   thawed if frozen*
10 teaspoons granulated or raw sugar

For the mousse:
¼ cup liqueur sugar syrup (page 22) flavored
*   with Grand Marnier, Raspberry eau de*
*   vie, Chambord, or other complementary*
*   liqueur*
1 cup diced rhubarb
1 tablespoon unflavored powdered gelatin
1 cup raspberry coulis (page 24)
1 cup low-fat (1%) cottage cheese, puréed
*   until very smooth*
½ cup yogurt cheese (page 23)
3 egg whites, at room temperature
¼ cup lemon, orange, or vanilla sugar
*   (page 21) or plain granulated sugar*

For serving:
1 cup (½ pint) raspberries
1½ cups raspberry coulis (page 24)

~To prepare the phyllo cornets, preheat an oven to 400° F. Line a baking sheet with parchment paper. Lightly spray 10 metal cream horn molds with the vegetable coating spray.

~Cut 1 phyllo sheet lengthwise into quarters, then cut each quarter in half crosswise, to create 8 strips in all. Lightly spray each strip with the vegetable coating spray. One at a time, wrap the strips around a cream horn mold until the entire surface of the mold is covered. Lightly spray the entire cornet again and sprinkle with 1 teaspoon of the sugar. Repeat this process using the remaining phyllo sheets and cream horn molds.

~Bake the cornets in the preheated oven until they are crisp and a light golden brown, 7 to 10 minutes. Remove from the oven and let cool just until they can be handled. Carefully push each cornet off the mold; do this gently so that you do not crush the phyllo. Let cool completely before filling (the cornets can be stored in a tightly covered container for up to 4 days).

~To prepare the mousse, combine the sugar syrup and rhubarb in a 1-quart saucepan and bring to a boil over high heat. Reduce the heat to low and simmer, uncovered, until the rhubarb is very soft, 3 to 5 minutes. Remove the pan from the heat and sprinkle the gelatin over the rhubarb. Return the pan to low heat and simmer gently, stirring constantly, until the gelatin dissolves, 1 to 2 minutes. Transfer the rhubarb mixture to a blender or a food processor fitted with a metal blade and purée until very smooth. Pour into a mixing bowl and add the raspberry coulis, puréed cottage cheese, and yogurt cheese. Using a balloon whisk or a large rubber spatula, mix together until smooth and well incorporated. Cover and chill until just barely beginning to set, about 1 hour.

~When the mixture is chilled to this point, place the egg whites in a grease-free bowl. Using a mixer set on medium speed, beat the egg whites until frothy. Increase the speed to high and beat until soft peaks form. Continuing to beat, add the sugar 1 tablespoon at a time, and beat until stiff, glossy peaks form.

~Using a balloon whisk or a large rubber spatula, fold one third of the egg whites into the rhubarb mixture to lighten it. Then gently fold the remaining egg whites into the mixture. Cover and chill until set, 4 to 6 hours.

~To assemble the dessert, drop 3 or 4 raspberries into the tip of each phyllo cornet. Spoon, or pipe using a pastry bag, a large dollop of the mousse into the cornet to fill it. Ladle 2 or 3 tablespoons of raspberry coulis onto each dessert plate, forming a pool. Lay a mousse-filled phyllo cornet on each pool. Spoon or pipe another dollop of mousse near the opening of the phyllo cornet and garnish with additional raspberries. Serve immediately.

Per serving: 140 calories
1 gram fat ~ 6.4% calories from fat

Italian Ricotta Cheesecake

~Anyone who loves the creamy, slightly grainy ricotta filling of classic Italian *cannoli* will enjoy this cheesecake. My husband tasted mountains of cheesecake for me as I attempted to combine the firm texture of ricotta with the delectable creaminess and subtle tang that characterizes the best cheesecakes. This deceptively low-fat version makes a wonderfully decadent, yet guilt-free breakfast. Drizzle sweet, dark purple blackberry coulis (page 24) on ice-cold slices of this cake, or serve with fresh peach slices that have been tossed with Amaretto. Heavenly.

Makes 12 servings

3 or 4 tablespoons amaretti *cookie crumbs*
   or graham cracker crumbs
2 eggs
2 cups low-fat (1%) cottage cheese
2 tablespoons freshly squeezed lemon juice
2 tablespoons freshly squeezed orange juice
Freshly grated zest of 1 orange
Freshly grated zest of 1 lemon
1 cup yogurt cheese (page 23)
⅓ cup lemon or vanilla sugar (page 21) or
   plain granulated sugar
1 teaspoon pure vanilla extract
1 teaspoon pure lemon extract
1 cup part-skim ricotta cheese
2 tablespoons all-purpose flour

~Preheat an oven to 325° F. Spray a 9- or 10-inch round cake pan lightly with a vegetable coating spray. Sprinkle the *amaretti* or graham cracker crumbs on the bottom and sides of the pan to coat completely.

~In a blender or in a food processor fitted with a metal blade, combine, in this order, the eggs, cottage cheese, orange and lemon juices, and orange and lemon zests. Blend until very smooth and creamy. Add the yogurt cheese, sugar, and vanilla and lemon extracts. Blend at a low speed until smooth and combined. Finally, add the ricotta cheese and flour and blend again until the batter achieves the smooth consistency of thick cream. Pour the batter through a fine-mesh sieve into a bowl (*not* the prepared pan) to remove any air bubbles, then carefully spoon the sieved batter into the prepared pan.

~Place the cake pan in a larger pan and pour in almost-boiling water to reach halfway up the sides to form a bain-marie. Bake in the preheated oven until barely firm in the center and slightly brown around the edges, 45 to 50 minutes. Remove the cheesecake from the oven and from the bain-marie and let cool on a wire rack for 1 hour.

~When the cake is cool, run a thin metal spatula around the edge of the cake to loosen it, if necessary, and then invert onto a serving plate. Lightly cover the cheesecake with plastic wrap and refrigerate until very cold, 4 hours or overnight. The cake will firm up as it chills.

Serve the cheesecake chilled, cut into wedges.

Per serving: 124 calories
2.2 grams fat ~ 16% calories from fat

FLORENCE

28

room to room, as if they were going to a dying's
art museum," said a connoisseur to me one day,
artichoke; it should be enjoyed, leaf by leaf."

Amaretti Peaches

~Here, ripe sweet summer peaches need only a light blanching to remove their skins and a quick baking to cook the meringue before serving. These are not only delicious and elegant, but also easy to prepare. To make the preparation even simpler, and to eliminate the need to heat the oven on a hot day, burnish the meringue with a hot blow torch. If you prefer to serve the peaches cold, pipe the meringue caps onto parchment paper-lined baking sheets, bake as directed, let cool, and slide atop the cold, stuffed peaches just before serving.

Makes 8 servings

juice of 1 lemon
4 large freestone peaches or nectarines
3 egg whites, at room temperature
½ teaspoon cream of tartar
pinch of salt
⅓ cup granulated sugar
32 raspberries
4 or 5 amaretti cookies, coarsely crumbled
For serving:
1 cup raspberry coulis (page 24)
raspberries

~Preheat an oven to 375° F. Line a baking sheet with parchment paper. Have ready a large bowl of ice water to which you have added the lemon juice.

~Fill a large pot with water, bring to a boil, and add the peaches. Count to 10, and, using a slotted spoon remove the peaches and immediately immerse them in the ice water. When the peaches are cool, slip off and discard their skins. Cut the peaches in half and remove and discard the pits. Return the peach halves to the ice water. If using nectarines instead of peaches, do not peel; simply cut in half and remove the pits.

~Place the egg whites in a large, grease-free bowl. Using a mixer set on medium speed, beat the egg whites until frothy. Add the cream of tartar and salt, increase the speed to high, and beat until soft peaks form. Add the sugar, 1 tablespoon at a time, and continue beating until stiff, glossy peaks form.

~Drain the peach halves and place on the prepared baking sheet, hollow sides up, or arrange the nectarine halves in the same manner. Fill each fruit cavity with 4 raspberries and some crumbled *amaretti.*

~Spoon the egg whites into a pastry bag fitted with a large star tip and pipe a meringue cap onto each stuffed fruit cavity, covering the filling completely.

~Bake in the preheated oven until the meringue is golden, 5 to 7 minutes. Remove from the oven and transfer to individual serving plates. Serve immediately, or let cool, cover, and refrigerate for up to 2 hours. To prevent the baked peaches from discoloring, brush the exposed fruit with freshly squeezed lemon juice before covering and chilling.

~To serve, ladle 2 or 3 tablespoons of the raspberry coulis onto each dessert plate. Place a peach or nectarine half onto each pool of coulis and garnish the plate with 3 or 4 raspberries.

Per serving: 80 calories
0.2 grams fat ~ 2.3% calories from fat

Banana-Rum Napoleons

~Prepare the phyllo pastry up to 1 day in advance to streamline the making of this dessert. Assemble the cream filling no more than a few hours ahead of serving to retain its flavor and freshness. If you are not a bananas-and-cream lover, substitute peach, nectarine, or any berry purée and flavor with the liqueur of your choice. Top the cream with fresh slices of the same fruit.

Makes 10 servings

For the pastry:
6 sheets phyllo dough (12 by 17 inches), thawed if frozen
butter-flavored vegetable coating spray
6 teaspoons granulated sugar

For the banana cream:
1¼ cups puréed banana (1½ to 2 large bananas)
1 to 2 tablespoons freshly squeezed lime juice
2½ tablespoons dark Jamaican rum
½ teaspoon pure vanilla extract
1¼ cups low-fat nondairy topping
4 medium bananas, sliced on the diagonal, ¼-inch thick
confectioners' sugar for topping

~First, prepare the pastry. Preheat an oven to 400° F. Line a baking sheet with parchment paper.

~Place 1 phyllo sheet on a flat work surface. Spray lightly with the butter-flavored vegetable coating spray and sprinkle with 1 teaspoon of the sugar. Place a second sheet of phyllo directly over the first, spray lightly with coating spray, and sprinkle with 1 teaspoon of the sugar. Repeat this process with a third phyllo sheet. Cut the layered phyllo into ten 6-by-3-inch rectangles. Discard any phyllo scraps. Place the rectangles on the prepared baking sheet and bake in the preheated oven until crisp and golden, 3 to 5 minutes. Watch carefully, as layered phyllo this thin can burn easily.

~Remove from the oven and transfer to a wire rack to cool completely. Repeat this process with the remaining 3 phyllo sheets and sugar, spraying each sheet with coating spray as you stack it. You will now have twenty 6-by-3 inch rectangles.

~To prepare the filling, place the puréed banana, lime juice, rum, vanilla extract, and nondairy topping in a mixing bowl. Using a balloon whisk or a large rubber spatula, fold together the ingredients until thoroughly incorporated. Cover and refrigerate the banana cream until serving time.

~Just before serving, place a phyllo rectangle on a dessert plate. Spoon ¼ cup of the banana cream onto the pastry and then top with 8 to 10 banana slices. Top the filling with a second phyllo rectangle, and sieve confectioners' sugar liberally over the top. Repeat this process with the remaining phyllo rectangles, filling, and banana slices. To create decorative marks on the top phyllo layer, heat a metal skewer over a gas flame or with a blow torch until very hot. Quickly lay the red-hot skewer on the sugar-coated phyllo to form a scorch mark. Make 3 or 4 marks on the top of each serving. Serve immediately.

Per serving: 105 calories
1.5 grams fat ~ 13% calories from fat

Candied Ginger Bavarians with Papaya-Passion Fruit Coulis and Strawberry Coulis

~Tangy fruit coulis balances the creamy texture and subtle, spicy taste in these Bavarians. Starting with the building block of vanilla bean crème anglaise, this recipe is a snap to prepare. French *darioles* are the perfect molds for these Bavarians. The small tinned steel molds come in cylindrical or tapered oval shapes and are used for a variety of molded desserts. They are available in many gourmet kitchen shops.

Makes 8 servings

1 recipe vanilla bean crème anglaise
    (see page 25)
one 2-inch-piece fresh ginger, peeled and
    grated
¼ cup apple juice
2 teaspoons unflavored powdered gelatin
3 egg whites, at room temperature
1 cup nonfat vanilla yogurt

For garnish:
1 or 2 passion fruits
1 cup papaya coulis (page 24)
8 teaspoons minced candied ginger
1 cup strawberry coulis (page 24)
8 strawberries
8 sprigs fresh mint

~Lightly spray eight 2-ounce metal dariole molds or decorative custard cups with a vegetable coating spray. Set aside.

~Prepare the crème anglaise as directed in the recipe, adding the fresh ginger to the milk at the same time as you add the vanilla bean. Pour the crème anglaise into a large bowl, cover, and chill thoroughly.

~Pour the apple juice into a small saucepan. Sprinkle the gelatin over the apple juice and let it soften for about 3 minutes. Place the saucepan over low heat and stir gently just until the gelatin dissolves completely, 1 to 2 minutes. Remove from the heat and set aside.

~Meanwhile, place the egg whites in a large, grease-free mixing bowl. Using a mixer set on medium speed, beat egg whites until frothy. Increase the speed to high and continue beating until stiff peaks form.

~Stir the yogurt into the chilled crème anglaise, then stir in the gelatin mixture. Using a balloon whisk or a large rubber spatula, fold one third of the egg whites into the crème anglaise to lighten it. Then gently fold the remaining egg whites into the crème anglaise mixture. Now spoon the mixture into the prepared molds, cover, and refrigerate until firm, about 4 hours. While the Bavarians are chilling, prepare the garnish.

~Cut the passion fruits in half and scoop out the pulp and seeds into a sieve placed over a bowl holding the papaya coulis.

Press the pulp and juice through the sieve into the coulis and then stir together. Discard the seeds.

~To serve, unmold each Bavarian onto an individual dessert plate. To do this, use your fingers to gently pull the Bavarian away from the edge of the mold to release the seal. The Bavarian should then slip out of the mold easily. Sprinkle each Bavarian with 1 teaspoon of the candied ginger. Spoon 2 tablespoons of the strawberry coulis around one side of the plate and 2 tablespoons of the papaya-passion fruit coulis around the other side. Garnish with a strawberry and a mint sprig.

Per serving: 95 calories
1.9 grams fat ~ 18% calories from fat

Ruby Pear Tart with Poire Williams Sabayon

~A lovely dessert that is spectacular to present, yet is surprisingly easy to prepare because the tart shell and the poached pears can be prepared a day ahead of serving. The pears develop a richer taste and deeper hue if allowed to steep in the poaching liquid overnight. Try an American pear brandy if French poire Williams is unavailable. Clear Creek Distilleries makes a fine one.

Makes 12 servings

For the pears:

1 can (12 ounces) cranberry juice
    concentrate
1½ cups red wine
1 cinnamon stick
4 or 5 whole cloves
2 or 3 strips lemon peel
½ vanilla bean
3 firm Bosc, Anjou, or similar pears (about
    1½ pounds), peeled, cored, and cut in
    half lengthwise

For the tart shell:

6 sheets phyllo dough (12 by 17 inches,
    thawed if frozen)
butter-flavored vegetable coating spray
4 teaspoons granulated sugar

For the sabayon:

1 egg
3 tablespoons granulated sugar
1 teaspoon cornstarch dissolved in
    1 tablespoon water
½ cup nonfat milk
3 tablespoons poire Williams
⅓ cup nonfat vanilla yogurt
1 pear half, canned in its own juice, drained
    and puréed (optional)
1 tablespoon granulated sugar for serving

~One day before serving the tart, prepare the pears. Combine the undiluted cranberry juice concentrate, red wine, cinnamon stick, cloves, and lemon peel in a 2-quart saucepan. Split the vanilla bean in half lengthwise and, using the tip of a sharp paring knife, scrape the seeds into the saucepan. Then add the pod halves as well. Bring to a boil and add the pear halves. Reduce the heat to low, cover, and poach the pears until they are barely softened when pierced, 7 to 10 minutes. Remove from the heat and let the pears cool in the poaching liquid to room temperature. Cover and chill in the liquid overnight. The pears will develop a dark ruby color the longer they soak in the poaching liquid.

~To prepare the tart shell, preheat the oven to 400° F. Line a baking sheet with parchment paper. Lay 1 phyllo sheet vertically on the prepared baking sheet. Spray lightly with the vegetable coating spray and sprinkle with ½ teaspoon of the granulated sugar. Lay a second sheet of phyllo dough directly over the first. Again spray lightly with coating spray and sprinkle with another ½ teaspoon sugar. Lay the third phyllo sheet horizontally across the center of the first 2 sheets. Spray lightly with coating spray and sprinkle it with ½ teaspoon sugar. Lay the fourth sheet diagonally atop the stack. Spray it with coating spray and sprinkle it with ½ teaspoon sugar. Now lay the fifth sheet on the stack, running it on the opposite diagonal so that the fourth and fifth sheets form an X and the stack is essentially a pastry round. Spray the sheet lightly with the vegetable spray and sprinkle with ½ teaspoon sugar. Lay the final phyllo sheet horizontally on the stack, as for the third sheet. Spray with vegetable coating spray and sprinkle with ½ teaspoon sugar (you will have used 1 tablespoon sugar in all). Starting from the outer edges of the phyllo sheets, carefully roll toward the center, creating an 8-inch round tart shell with a 1- to 1½-inch high rim. Pierce the bottom of the tart shell in a few places with the tines of a fork. Spray the entire tart shell very lightly with coating spray and sprinkle the rim with the remaining 1 teaspoon sugar. Bake the tart shell on the prepared baking sheet in the preheated oven until crisp and golden brown, 7 to 10 minutes. Remove from the oven and let cool completely. The tart shell can be made 1 day in advance of serving and stored, covered, in a cool, dry place.

(continued on page 44)

~To prepare the sabayon, combine the egg and sugar in a small metal or other heat-proof bowl. Place the bowl in a sauté pan filled halfway with simmering water and whisk continuously until sugar crystals dissolve and the mixture thickens and is hot to the touch (120° F), 1 to 2 minutes. Whisk in the dissolved cornstarch, milk and poire Williams and continue to whisk over the heat until thickened, 2 or 3 minutes. Remove the bowl from the heat and beat using a hand-held mixer set on low speed or a large balloon whisk, until the mixture is thick, light, and cool to the touch. Fold in the yogurt. Taste the mixture, and if you desire a stronger pear taste, fold in the puréed pear half. Cover and chill well.

~Just before serving time, assemble the tart. Preheat a broiler. Drain the pear halves. Leave them whole, or slice them, leaving the slices attached at the stem and fanning out the slices slightly. Spread the sabayon over the bottom of the tart shell and arrange the pears on top, facing the pointed end of each pear half toward the center of the tart. Sprinkle any exposed sabayon with the 1 tablespoon sugar and place the tart under the preheated broiler to caramelize the sugar, 30 to 60 seconds. Alternatively, use a blow torch set at a medium flame to caramelize the sugar. Serve immediately, cut into wedges.

Per serving: 150 calories
0.7 grams fat ~ 4% calories from fat

Sandy Cake with Tea-Berry Compote

~This unusual torte is made with a mixture of semolina and ground almonds for a pleasantly chewy texture. Look for the semolina in speciality-food shops or health-food stores. The delicate, flowery taste of the tea-flavored berry compote gives this novel dessert a wonderful flavor. Pitted cherries are also a good addition to the berry mixture.

Makes 10 servings

For the cake:
3 eggs, separated and at room temperature
½ cup lemon sugar (page 21) or plain
 granulated sugar
1 tablespoon freshly grated lemon zest
2 tablespoons freshly squeezed lemon juice
⅓ cup fine semolina
5 heaping tablespoons (1 ounce) ground
 almonds
1 teaspoon pure almond extract
⅛ teaspoon salt

For the tea-berry compote:
½ cup brewed Darjeeling, herbal, mint,
 or other delicately scented tea
¼ cup granulated sugar
2 cups (1 pint) mixed berries such as
 raspberries, blueberries, blackberries,
 loganberries, and strawberries
Confectioners' sugar for topping

~Preheat an oven to 350° F. Lightly spray an 8-inch round cake pan or a 5-by-9-by-3-inch loaf pan with a vegetable coating spray.

~To prepare the cake, in a bowl beat the egg yolks with ¼ cup of the sugar until thick and lemon colored, 2 to 3 minutes. Fold in the lemon zest, and juice, semolina, ground almonds, and almond extract. Set aside. Place the egg whites in a separate, grease-free bowl. Using a hand-held mixer set on medium speed, beat the egg whites until frothy. Add the salt, increase the speed to high, and beat until soft peaks form. Add the remaining ¼ cup sugar, 1 tablespoon at a time, and continue beating until stiff, glossy peaks form.

~Using a balloon whisk or a large rubber spatula, fold one third of the egg whites into the semolina batter to lighten it. Then, carefully fold the remaining egg whites into the batter. Spoon the batter into the prepared pan. Bake the cake in the preheated oven until firm to the touch and golden, 18 to 22 minutes. Remove from the oven and cool on a wire rack for 5 minutes. Run a thin metal spatula around the ends of the cake to loosen it and then invert onto the rack to cool completely.

~While the cake is baking, prepare the compote. Combine the tea and sugar in a small saucepan over medium heat. Bring to a boil and cook, stirring, until the sugar dissolves. Remove from the heat and let cool completely.

~Place the berries in a bowl, add the cooled tea syrup, and toss well. Cover and chill thoroughly.

~Transfer the cooled cake to a serving plate. Sieve the confectioners' sugar over the top. Cut into slices and serve with the tea-berry compote on the side or spooned over the top of the cake.

Per serving: 115 calories
2.9 grams fat ~ 23% calories from fat

Pear Soufflé with Late-Harvest Riesling

~The delicate pear taste and light texture of this soufflé is enhanced by the rich, fruity flavor of a late-harvest Riesling. Serve small glasses of the same wine along with the soufflé.

Makes 8 servings

granulated sugar for soufflé dish
¾ cup pear butter (page 23)
¼ cup late-harvest Riesling
4 egg whites, at room temperature
¼ teaspoon cream of tartar
½ cup granulated sugar
2 teaspoons cornstarch

~Preheat an oven to 350° F. Spray a 1-quart soufflé dish lightly with a vegetable coating spray. Sprinkle granulated sugar on the bottom and sides of dish to form a light coating.

~In a bowl combine the pear butter and wine and stir together until smooth. Place the egg whites in a separate, grease-free bowl. Using a mixer set at medium speed, beat until frothy. Add the cream of tartar, increase the speed to high, and continue beating until soft peaks form. Add the ½ cup sugar, 1 tablespoon at a time, and continue beating until stiff, glossy peaks form.

~Using a balloon whisk or a large rubber spatula, fold one third of the egg whites into the pear mixture to lighten it. Sift the cornstarch over the pear mixture and fold in. Finally, gently fold the remaining egg whites into the pear mixture.

~Spoon the batter into the prepared dish. Bake the soufflé in the preheated oven until puffy and golden and barely soft in the center, 20 to 25 minutes. Remove from the oven and serve immediately.

Per serving: 103 calories
0 grams fat ~ 0% calories from fat

Raspberry Cheesecake Beggars' Purses

~Traditional savory beggars' purses are stuffed with crème fraîche and caviar. Here is a sweet version featuring a creamy cheesecake filling spiked with lemon and laced with fresh berries. Serve these little bundles cold with a contrasting fruit coulis (page 24), such as kiwi, or with honey-yogurt sauce (page 22) or additional berries. If desired, substitute blackberries, blueberries, or chunks of ripe nectarine for the raspberries.

Makes 8 servings

2 cups low-fat (1%) cottage cheese
½ cup nonfat plain yogurt
2 eggs
½ cup plain granulated sugar or lemon or
*   vanilla sugar (page 21)*
½ teaspoon pure vanilla extract
¼ teaspoon pure lemon extract
grated zest of 1 lemon
¼ cup freshly squeezed lemon juice
1 teaspoon cornstarch
1 tablespoon all-purpose flour
1 cup raspberries
8 crêpes (page 27)
confectioners' sugar for topping

~Preheat an oven to 325° F. Spray an 8-inch square baking pan lightly with a vegetable coating spray.

~In a food processor fitted with a metal blade or in a blender, combine the cottage cheese, yogurt, eggs, granulated sugar, vanilla and lemon extracts, lemon zest and juice, cornstarch, and flour. Blend until smooth and creamy. Pour into the prepared baking pan and carefully stir in the raspberries. Place the baking pan in a larger pan and add almost-boiling water to reach halfway up the sides of the cake pan, to form a bain-marie. Bake in the preheated oven until the cheesecake is firm and jiggles only slightly in the center, 30 to 45 minutes.

~Remove from the oven and bain-marie and let cool to room temperature. Cover and chill thoroughly, at least 4 hours or overnight. Meanwhile, make the crêpes.

~To assemble the purses cut a ¼-inch-wide strip from the edge of each crêpe. Set the strips aside. Spoon one-eighth of the cheesecake filling into the center of each crêpe and draw the edges of the crêpe up and around the filling to form a small parcel. Carefully pinch the top closed. Wrap a crêpe strip around the neck of each parcel to secure it closed. Nothing more than the natural moisture of the crêpe and a little pressure is needed to adhere the crêpe strips to the necks of the parcels. Using scissors or a small sharp knife, evenly trim off the top of each parcel above the neck. Cover the parcels loosely with plastic wrap and chill until ready to serve, up to 2 hours.

~Just before serving, sieve confectioners' sugar over each bundle.

Per serving: 160 calories
3 grams fat ~ 17% calories from fat

Strawberry Bavarian Cake

~A butter-free *génoise* forms the base for this light fruit-filled cake. You may present this cake as a single 9-inch round cake or as individual 3-inch round cakes. Don't be limited to using strawberry coulis; any fruit coulis can flavor the Bavarian. Fresh flowers are an attractive garnish. It is important to use only pesticide-free, non-toxic edible flowers. If you are uncertain about any flower, check with a local purveyor of edible flowers or a gourmet shop or garnish with fresh fruit such as kiwifruit, strawberry or peach slices, small clusters of red currants, or whole berries. Accompany the cake with fruit coulis, if desired.

Makes 12 servings

One 9-by-13-inch butter-free génoise
    roulade (page 26)
*¼ cup liqueur sugar syrup (page 22) flavored
    with Grand Marnier*

For the filling:
2 cups strawberry coulis (page 24)
1 tablespoon unflavored powdered gelatin
*1 cup fromage frais (page 23) or yogurt
    cheese (page 23)*
2 tablespoons Grand Marnier
1 teaspoon freshly grated orange zest
3 egg whites, at room temperature
*⅓ cup orange sugar (page 21) or plain
    granulated sugar*
Nontoxic flower petals or fresh fruit for garnish

~Bake the *génoise* roulade and let it cool completely. Remove the bottom of a 9- or 10-inch springform pan and use it as a template. Place it on the roulade and cut out a cake round the same size. Reattach the pan sides to the springform bottom and place the cake round in the pan. If you are preparing miniature cakes, line a baking sheet with parchment paper. Cut out twelve 3-inch rounds from the *génoise* using a 3-inch round open-topped biscuit or cookie cutter. Now place twelve 3-inch round biscuit cutters on the prepared baking sheet and line the bottoms of the cutters with the cake rounds.

~Tear off a piece of the remaining *génoise* to make crumbs to use for the garnish. Place it in a food processor fitted with a metal blade and process to form soft crumbs. You will need about ½ cup crumbs. Wrap and freeze any remaining *génoise* for future use. Set the crumbs aside.

~Using a pastry brush, soak the cake circle(s) with the sugar syrup. You want the cake(s) to be moist but not soggy. If the *génoise* is very fresh, you may not need all of the syrup. Discard any unused syrup.

~To prepare the filling, pour ½ cup of the strawberry coulis into a small saucepan and sprinkle with the gelatin. Let the gelatin soften for about 3 minutes. Place the saucepan over low heat and stir gently just until the gelatin dissolves completely, 1 to 2 minutes. Transfer the strawberry-gelatin mixture and the remaining 1½ cups strawberry coulis to a large mixing bowl. Using a balloon whisk or a large rubber spatula, fold the fromage frais or yogurt cheese, Grand Marnier, and orange zest into the strawberry coulis until thoroughly incorporated. Cover the bowl and refrigerate until just barely beginning to set, about 1 hour.

~When the mixture is chilled to this point, place the egg whites in a large, grease-free bowl. Using a mixer set at medium speed, beat the egg whites until frothy. Increase the speed to high and beat until soft peaks form. Add the sugar, 1 tablespoon at a time, and continue beating until stiff, glossy peaks form.

~Using a balloon whisk or a large rubber spatula, fold one third of the egg whites into the strawberry mixture to lighten it. Then gently fold the remaining egg whites into the mixture. Spoon the Bavarian mixture into the large cake pan, or divide it among the ten smaller molds. Smooth the tops with a large metal spatula. Cover the cake(s) lightly with plastic wrap and refrigerate until set, 4-6 hours.

~To serve, use your fingers to pull the cake(s) gently away from the edge of the mold(s) to release the seal. Unclasp and remove the springform pan sides, or slip the 3-inch rings from around the small cakes. Pat the reserved crumbs around the sides of the cake(s) and place on a serving dish. Garnish the top(s) with flower petals or fresh fruit. Serve the miniature cakes whole and the large cake cut into wedges.

*Per serving: 150 calories
2 grams fat ~ 13% calories from fat*

Old-Fashioned Endings

Sometimes an exotically flavored, elaborate dessert is not what we crave. Instead we want desserts that remind us of the way the kitchen smelled when we came home from school to cookies fresh from the oven. We want desserts that are a part of everyday life — not dinner-party creations designed to impress, but homey desserts that bring back memories. These are comforting desserts whether eaten alone sitting in a big rocking chair while balancing a good book and an overinterested cat, or enjoyed in a lively family setting with everyone clamoring for the largest piece.

~Old-fashioned desserts are redolent with familiar spices and fruits. Some are perfect served warm, straight from the oven, such as the molasses-rich pumpkin gingerbread or fresh pineapple upside-down cake. Classic treats such as lemon-poppy seed strawberry short-cake soothe cranky tempers on blisteringly hot summer days. These desserts are childhood favorites, familiar and accessible in their simplicity yet rich in memory-provoking flavors. Unfortunately, such desserts are normally high in fat, particularly because of the liberal use of butter. It is possible to capture the rich flavors of these popular sweets without the butter, however, by following a few simple fat-reducing techniques.

~Whether your childhood was two years ago or twenty, these updated old-fashioned desserts will satisfy your nostalgic sweet tooth without sacrificing your waistline.

Pumpkin Gingerbread

~The best gingerbread cake I ever made was for a traditional tea during my first week at the Cordon Bleu. To make that incredibly moist and spicy cake, we used lots of butter, brown sugar, and treacle, the thickest, blackest syrup I had ever seen. Blackstrap molasses is more commonly found in the United States, however, so I have used it here, along with honey and pumpkin purée to make this moist and flavorful version of that highly fattening classic. Liquid sweeteners and fruit or vegetable purées act as humectants, drawing moisture from the environment to keep cakes moist, thereby eliminating the need for a lot of fat to do the same thing. Serve this delicious gingerbread with applesauce, or with sautéed apple slices over a scoop of vanilla frozen yogurt or ice milk.

Makes 10 servings

2 tablespoons canola oil or other vegetable oil
¼ cup blackstrap molasses
¼ cup honey
1 whole egg plus 1 egg white
¾ cup canned pumpkin purée
½ cup buttermilk
1¼ cups all-purpose flour
1 teaspoon baking soda
¼ teaspoon salt
2 teaspoons ground ginger
1 teaspoon ground cinnamon
¼ teaspoon ground nutmeg
⅛ teaspoon ground white pepper

~Preheat an oven to 350° F. Spray a 4- or 5-cup bundt or kugelhopf pan lightly with a vegetable coating spray.

~In a small bowl whisk together the oil, molasses, honey, eggs and egg white, pumpkin, and buttermilk until smooth. In a separate bowl sift together the flour, baking soda, salt, ginger, cinnamon, nutmeg, and white pepper. Make a well in the center of the dry ingredients and pour the wet ingredients into it. Whisk the ingredients together until smooth.

~Pour the batter into the prepared pan. Bake the cake in the preheated oven until a thin wooden skewer inserted in the center comes out clean, 25 to 30 minutes. Remove from the oven and let cool on a wire rack for about 5 minutes. Then invert the cake onto the rack, lift off the pan, and let cool completely before slicing.

Per serving: 130 calories
3.6 grams fat ~ 25% calories from fat

Bavarian Apple Strudel

~The first words I learned in German—and the only ones I still remember—are *Kaffee mit Schlag*. In Viennese coffee houses where I repeated those words I was always rewarded with wonderfully rich coffee topped with billows of whipped cream. Warm apple strudel dusted with a thick coat of confectioners' sugar was a natural accompaniment. Here, phyllo pastry provides a wonderfully crisp foil for the warm fruit filling. A vegetable coating spray makes a successful substitute for the highly caloric melted butter commonly used to keep the thin layers of phyllo separated and flaky during baking. Partner a slice of this strudel with a "skinny" *caffe latte* made with nonfat milk. It tastes surprisingly rich!

Makes 12 servings

¼ cup apple juice concentrate
1 tablespoon plus 1 teaspoon vanilla sugar
   (page 21) or plain granulated sugar
1 teaspoon ground cinnamon
¼ teaspoon ground nutmeg
pinch of ground cloves
2 large green cooking apples such as Pippin
   or Granny Smith, peeled, cored, and
   sliced lengthwise
1 large Golden Delicious apple, peeled, cored
   and sliced lengthwise

3 tablespoons amaretti *or* crisp gingersnap
   cookie crumbs
7 sheets phyllo dough (12 by 17 inches),
   thawed if frozen
butter-flavored vegetable coating spray
confectioners' sugar for topping

~Preheat an oven to 400° F.

~Combine the undiluted apple juice concentrate and the 1 tablespoon sugar in a 10- or 12-inch sauté pan and place over medium heat. Bring to a boil and add the cinnamon, nutmeg, and cloves. Boil until thick and syrupy, 1 to 2 minutes. Add the apples and cook over medium heat, stirring occasionally, until tender when pierced with a fork but not mushy, 2 or 3 minutes. Remove from the heat and stir in 1 tablespoon of the *amaretti* or gingersnap crumbs. Cool to room temperature.

~Lay 1 phyllo sheet on an ungreased baking sheet, with a long side facing you. Spray lightly with the butter-flavored vegetable coating spray and sprinkle with 1 teaspoon of the crumbs. Top with a second phyllo sheet. Repeat this process with the remaining phyllo sheets and cookie crumbs, ending with a phyllo sheet. Place the cooled apple filling along the edge of the phyllo dough nearest you, leaving a ½-inch border at each end. Then roll up the pastry, jelly-roll fashion. When the roll is completed, pinch the ends closed. Spray lightly on all sides with the vegetable coating spray and then sprinkle on all sides with the remaining 1 teaspoon sugar.

~Bake the strudel on the baking sheet in the preheated oven until the pastry is golden brown and the filling is hot and bubbly, 20 to 30 minutes. Remove from the oven and let cool slightly. Sieve confectioners' sugar over the top, slice, and serve.

Per serving: 64 calories
0.4 grams fat ~ 5.6% calories from fat

Blueberry Crisps

~Both the crumbly topping and the fruit filling can be prepared in advance. Best served warm, these crisps can bake while you serve dinner. Top them, warm from the oven, with a small scoop of vanilla ice cream, frozen yogurt, or ice milk or with a dusting of confectioners sugar.

Makes 8 servings

For the topping:
1 cup old-fashioned rolled oats
8 amaretti *cookies, coarsely chopped*
¼ *teaspoon ground nutmeg*
½ *teaspoon ground cinnamon*
2 *tablespoons honey*
1 *tablespoon low-calorie margarine, melted*

For the filling:
4 cups (2 pints) fresh or thawed,
    unsweetened, frozen blueberries
1 lemon
1 tablespoon granulated sugar or honey
1 tablespoon cornstarch dissolved in
    2 tablespoons water

~To prepare the topping, heat an oven to 350° F. Combine all the ingredients in a bowl and stir until the honey and margarine coat the oats and cookies thoroughly. Spread the mixture on a baking sheet and bake in the preheated oven until golden and the syrup starts to thicken, 10 to 15 minutes. Remove from the oven and let cool completely. As the topping cools it will become crisp.

~Meanwhile, to prepare the filling, place 3 cups of the berries in a saucepan. Grate the zest from the lemon and add it to the pan. Then juice the lemon and add the juice along with the sugar or honey. Cover, place over medium heat, and cook at a gentle boil until the berries are soft, bubbling, and juicy, about 10 minutes. Add the cornstarch mixture, bring back to a boil, and boil, stirring constantly, for 1 to 2 minutes. Remove from the heat and stir in the remaining 1 cup berries. Cover and chill if not using immediately.

~If the oven is not already set at 350° F, preheat it to that temperature. Spray eight 2-ounce ramekins lightly with a vegetable coating spray. Spoon the filling into the ramekins, dividing it equally among them. Divide the topping among them as well, sprinkling it evenly over the berry filling. Arrange the ramekins on a baking sheet and bake in the preheated oven until the filling is hot and bubbly, 10 to 15 minutes. Remove the berry crisps from the oven and serve warm.

Per serving: 130 calories
1.9 grams fat ~ 13% calories from fat

Fresh Pineapple Upside-Down Cake

~Traditionally, pineapple upside-down cake is made with a gooey syrup of brown sugar and butter that candies the pineapple as it bakes. Here is an updated version that uses a similarly sweet, but fat-free syrup to bathe the pineapple. This syrup emphasizes rather than diminishes the sweet-tart flavor of the fresh fruit. If using fresh pineapple, be sure to use a ripe one, as no amount of cooking will completely tenderize an underripe fruit.

Makes 8 servings

For the pineapple topping:
2 tablespoons light brown sugar
¼ cup apple juice concentrate
½ teaspoon ground nutmeg
½ teaspoon ground cinnamon
pinch of ground cloves
2 heaping cups fresh, ripe pineapple chunks,
    or well-drained pineapple chunks canned
    in their own juice.
1 teaspoon cornstarch dissolved in ½ cup
    pineapple juice

For the génoise layer:
3 eggs
⅓ cup granulated sugar
pinch of ground cardamom
1 teaspoon pure vanilla extract
½ teaspoon pure coconut extract
⅔ cup cake flour, sifted twice
pinch of salt
confectioners' sugar for topping

~Preheat an oven to 350° F. To prepare the topping, combine the sugar and undiluted apple juice concentrate in a 10- or 12-inch sauté pan and place over medium heat. Bring to a boil and add the spices. Boil until thick and syrupy, 1 to 2 minutes. Add the pineapple chunks and cook, stirring occasionally, until the fruit is tender and translucent. The riper the pineapple, the faster it will cook; ripe pineapple usually takes 4 to 5 minutes. Using a slotted spoon, remove the fruit from the sauté pan and set aside in a dish. Leave the cooking juices in the pan, add the cornstarch mixture and bring to a boil. Boil, stirring constantly, until thickened, 1 to 2 minutes. Add this sauce to the reserved pineapple.

~Spray a 9- or 10-inch round cake pan lightly with a vegetable coating spray. Pour the pineapple mixture into the pan, using a small spoon or spatula to spread the fruit evenly over the pan bottom.

~To prepare the *génoise*, combine the eggs, sugar, and spice in a large metal or other heatproof bowl. Place the bowl in a large sauté pan filled halfway with simmering water and whisk continuously until the sugar crystals dissolve and the mixture thickens and is hot to the touch (120° F.), 3 to 4 minutes. Remove the bowl from the water and beat the batter with the whisk attachment of a mixer set on high speed until it triples in volume and the bowl is cool to the touch, about 5 minutes. Beat in the vanilla and coconut extracts. Sift flour and salt together. Using a balloon whisk or large rubber spatula, gently fold the flour, one-third at a time, into the batter.

~Carefully spoon the cake batter over the pineapple: try not to disturb the fruit. Bake the cake in the preheated oven until puffed and golden and a thin wooden skewer inserted in the center comes out clean, 20 to 25 minutes. Remove from the oven. Run a thin metal spatula around the edge of the cake and carefully invert onto a serving platter. Sieve confectioners' sugar over the top and serve warm.

Per serving: 140 calories
2.4 grams fat ~ 15% calories from fat

Apple and Dried Sour Cherry Turnovers

~Tangy dried cherries, which can be found in health-food or specialty-food shops, are becoming serious rivals to raisins in cooking or just for eating out of hand. Combined with apples they make a flavorful filling for this phyllo pastry dessert. Prepare a few batches of these turnovers and freeze them, unbaked. Then, for a quick, hot dessert, pop them directly from the freezer into the oven. Serve warm sprinkled with confectioners' sugar or with a scoop or two of frozen vanilla yogurt.

Makes 8 servings

4 large, cooking apples such as Pippin, Granny Smith, or Jonathan, peeled, cored, and diced
¼ cup vanilla sugar syrup (page 22)
¼ teaspoon ground cinnamon
1 teaspoon cornstarch dissolved in 1 tablespoon water
¼ cup dried sour cherries
6 sheets phyllo dough (12 by 17 inches), thawed if frozen
butter-flavored vegetable coating spray
6 teaspoons granulated sugar
1 tablespoon granulated sugar mixed with 1 teaspoon cinnamon
confectioners' sugar for topping (optional)

~Preheat an oven to 400° F.

~In a saucepan combine the apples, vanilla syrup, and cinnamon. Cover and cook over medium heat until the apples are tender, 4 to 5 minutes. Stir the cornstarch mixture into the apples and bring to a boil. Cook until thickened, about 1 minute. Remove from the heat and stir in the dried cherries. Let cool completely before making turnovers.

~Lay 1 phyllo sheet on a flat work surface. Spray lightly with the vegetable coating spray and sprinkle with 1 teaspoon of the sugar. Place a second phyllo sheet directly over the first, spraying it lightly with a vegetable coating spray and sprinkling it with 1 teaspoon of the sugar. Repeat with

(continued on page 58)

a third sheet of phyllo dough. Cut the layered phyllo into four 6-inch squares. Discard any phyllo scraps. Repeat this process with the remaining 3 phyllo sheets and 3 teaspoons sugar. You will have eight 6-inch squares in all.

~Spoon ¼ cup of the cooled apple filling onto the corner of a phyllo square; do not place it too near the edge. Fold the opposite corner of the square over the filling to create a triangle-shaped turnover. Seal the turnover closed by folding over a ¼-inch rim around the edge of the pastry. Repeat this process with the remaining pastry squares and filling.

~Sprinkle each turnover with a little of the cinnamon-sugar mixture and arrange them on an ungreased baking sheet. Bake the turnovers in the preheated oven until the pastry is crisp and golden and the filling is hot, about 15 minutes. Remove from the oven and sieve confectioners' sugar over the top, if desired. Serve warm.

Per serving: 120 calories
0.4 grams fat ~ 3% calories from fat

French Apple Tarts

~Apple butter and Calvados strengthen the bold apple flavor of these tarts. The low-fat pastry remains tender due to the use of cottage cheese in the dough. Best served warm, these tarts can be baked ahead of time. Do not glaze them, however. Let them cool and then rewarm them in the oven and brush with the glaze just before serving.

Makes 8 servings

1 recipe flaky pastry (page 27)
2 large Golden Delicious apples
8 teaspoons apple butter (page 24)
8 teaspoons Calvados or other apple brandy
whole nutmeg for grating
¼ cup apricot jam
1 tablespoon freshly squeezed lemon juice or
   water
8 teaspoons granulated sugar

~Preheat the oven to 350° F. Prepare the pastry dough. On a lightly floured board, roll out the dough about ¼ inch thick. Cut out eight 3-inch rounds. Line a baking sheet with parchment paper. Place the pastry rounds on the sheet and prick each round in a few places with the tines of a fork. Chill the pastry for 15 minutes.

~While the pastry is chilling, peel and core the apples and cut them lengthwise into very thin slices.

~Spread 1 teaspoon of the apple butter over the surface of each pastry round, leaving a ¼-inch border uncovered. Arrange one eighth of the apple slices atop each pastry round and sprinkle 1 teaspoon of the Calvados over each. Grate a little nutmeg over each tart. Bake the tarts in the preheated oven until the pastry is crisp and brown and the apples are tender, 20 to 25 minutes.

~While the tarts are baking, prepare a glaze by combining the jam and the lemon juice or water in a small saucepan. Place over medium heat until the jam liquefies, then pass it through a fine-mesh sieve to remove any fruit chunks. Return the glaze to the pan and reheat gently just before using.

~Remove the tarts from the oven. Preheat a broiler. Sprinkle each tart with 1 teaspoon of the sugar and place under the broiler for a few seconds to caramelize the sugar. Remove the tarts from the broiler, brush the warm glaze over the fruit, and serve warm.

Per serving: 168 calories
4.5 grams fat ~ 25% calories from fat

Lemon-Poppy Seed Strawberry Shortcake

~My father is a fireman and on every Fourth of July while I was growing up, he took charge of the family's backyard fireworks display. My brothers and I wrote our names in the sky with burning sparklers as he lined up the brightly colored cones and cylinders, saving the most glittering and extravagant display for the grand finale. Exotically named "The Silver Spangler," "Mystery Geyser," and "Tower of Jewels," they stood at attention like smartly dressed soldiers wrapped in purple, silver, and gold finery.

~No dessert heralds this all-American holiday better than fresh strawberry shortcake. My mother made her own version, with our choice of whipped cream or vanilla ice cream to accompany the berries and cake. If we were feeling particularly gluttonous, we had both, stirring the crushed berries into the ice cream and topping off the whole delicious mass with huge mounds of freshly whipped cream.

~Not as fattening, but just as delicious, my version of this classic dessert has a tangy lemon flavor and pleasant poppy-seed crunch to complement its moist texture. If you like, crush some of the berries to release their juices and stir them into the frozen yogurt. Slice the remaining berries to crown the finished shortcake.

Makes 12 servings

For the shortcake:
4 eggs
½ cup lemon sugar (page 21) or plain
    granulated sugar
grated zest of 1 lemon
1 teaspoon pure vanilla extract
½ teaspoon pure lemon extract
¼ cup freshly squeezed lemon juice
1 cup cake flour, sifted twice
pinch of salt
4 teaspoons poppy seeds

For the filling:
4 cups (2 pints) strawberries, hulled
2 tablespoons vanilla sugar syrup or liqueur
    sugar syrup flavored with Framboise or
    Grand Marnier (page 21)
2 tablespoons freshly squeezed orange juice
1½ pints soft-serve, nonfat vanilla frozen
    yogurt
confectioners' sugar for topping

~Preheat an oven to 350° F. Select a 5-by-9-by-3-inch loaf pan, a 12-well cupcake pan, or a 9-inch round cake pan. Spray lightly with a vegetable coating spray.

~To prepare the shortcake, combine the eggs, sugar, and lemon zest in a metal or other heatproof bowl. Place the bowl in a large sauté pan filled halfway with simmering water and whisk continuously until the sugar crystals dissolve and the mixture thickens slightly and is hot to the touch (120° F), 3 to 4 minutes. Remove the bowl from the water and beat the egg mixture with the whisk attachment of a mixer set on high speed until it triples in volume and the bowl is cool to the touch, about 5 minutes. Beat in the vanilla and lemon extracts and lemon juice, 1 tablespoon at a time. Sift the cake flour, salt, and poppy seeds together. Using a balloon whisk or a large rubber spatula, fold the flour mixture, one third at a time, carefully into the batter.

~Spoon the batter into the prepared pan. If using a cupcake pan, fill the wells two-thirds full. Bake in the preheated oven until puffed and golden and a thin wooden skewer inserted in the center of the cake comes out clean, 15 to 18 minutes (cupcakes may take less time). Remove from the oven and invert the cake or cupcakes onto a wire rack, lift off the pan, and let cool completely.

~Just before serving, prepare the filling. Slice the berries lengthwise into a bowl, or, for a juicier shortcake, crush half the berries and slice the other half. Add the sugar syrup and orange juice, and toss well. Slice the cake and place on individual dessert plates. Top each portion with an equal amount of the frozen yogurt and of the berries. Sieve confectioners' sugar over the top and serve.

Per serving: 152 calories
2.5 grams fat ~ 15% calories from fat

Apricot Cobbler

~The house where I grew up is surrounded by apricot trees. Every summer my brothers and I would gather the ripest apricots that had fallen to the ground and carry them to the kitchen for my mother. I remember her making jar after jar of jam and mountains of dried apricots and fruit leather for the winter ahead. Sometimes, in the mornings before the house became too hot, she would make apricot cobbler, my brother Adam's favorite. Here is my lower-fat adaptation of her cakelike cobbler.

Makes 10 servings

For the fruit filling:
⅓ cup granulated sugar
¼ cup water
2 or 3 strips lemon zest
2 pounds apricots, cut in half and pitted
1 teaspoon ground cinnamon

For the génoise:
3 eggs
⅓ cup granulated sugar
¼ teaspoon ground cinnamon
¼ teaspoon ground nutmeg
1 teaspoon pure vanilla extract
⅔ cup cake flour, sifted twice

~Preheat an oven to 350° F. Spray a 12-inch-long oval gratin dish or similar dish lightly with a vegetable coating spray.

~To prepare the filling, combine the sugar, water, and lemon zest in a heavy-bottomed saucepan over medium heat. Bring to a boil, stirring to dissolve the sugar. Reduce the heat to medium and add the apricot halves. Cook gently, stirring occasionally, until the apricots are soft but some of them retain their shape. Remove from the heat, stir in the cinnamon, and let cool to room temperature.

~To prepare the *génoise*, combine the eggs, sugar, cinnamon, and nutmeg in a large metal or other heatproof bowl. Place the bowl in a large sauté pan filled halfway with simmering water and whisk continuously until the sugar crystals dissolve and the mixture thickens and is hot to the touch (about 120°), 4 to 5 minutes. Remove the bowl from the water and beat the egg mixture with the whisk attachment of a mixer set on high speed until it triples in volume and the bowl is cool to the touch, about 5 minutes. Beat in the vanilla extract. Using a balloon whisk or a large rubber spatula, gently fold the cake flour into the batter, one third at a time, being careful not to deflate the mixture.

~Spoon the cake batter into the prepared dish. Remove the lemon zest from the cooled apricots and spoon them over the cake batter until most of the batter is covered.

~Bake the cobbler in the preheated oven until firm and golden and the top springs back to the touch (cake will rise and cover the apricots), 20 to 30 minutes. Serve warm, at room temperature, or chilled.

Per serving: 135 calories
1.8 grams fat ~ 12% calories from fat

Banana Cake

~Use very ripe bananas for their natural sweetness and walnut oil for a hint of nutty flavor.

Makes 10 servings

2 tablespoons walnut oil or canola oil
¼ cup firmly packed dark brown sugar
¼ cup granulated sugar
1 whole egg plus 1 egg white
1 cup puréed banana
½ cup nonfat plain yogurt
1 teaspoon pure vanilla extract
1¼ cups all-purpose flour
½ teaspoon baking powder
½ teaspoon baking soda
¼ teaspoon salt
confectioners' sugar for topping (optional)

~Preheat an oven to 350° F. Spray an 8-inch round cake pan or a 4- or 5-cup bundt or kugelhopf pan with a vegetable coating spray.

~In a mixing bowl stir together the oil, sugars, whole egg, egg white, banana, yogurt, and vanilla extract until smooth. In a separate bowl sift together the flour, baking powder, baking soda, and salt. Make a well in the center of the dry ingredients and pour the wet ingredients into it. Using a wooden spoon or rubber spatula, gradually stir together all the ingredients until smooth.

(continued on page 64)

~Pour the batter into the prepared pan. Bake the cake on the middle rack of the preheated oven until it is firm and golden and a thin skewer inserted in the center comes out with only a few moist crumbs clinging to it, 25 to 35 minutes. Remove from the oven to a wire rack for a few minutes. Then invert the cake onto the rack, lift off the pan, and let cool completely. Just before serving, sieve confectioners' sugar over the top, if desired.

Per serving: 155 calories
3.6 grams fat ~ 20% calories from fat

Blueberry Blintzes

~These flavorful blintzes are as luscious and satisfying as their higher-fat counterparts. Frozen blueberries are a successful substitute for fresh berries in this recipe, enabling you to enjoy this dessert year-round. If you prefer, eliminate the compote and sprinkle the cheese blintzes with confectioners' sugar and a dollop of fresh peach, strawberry, or raspberry preserves.

Makes 8 servings

For the blueberry compote:
2 cups fresh or thawed, frozen unsweetened
   blueberries
grated zest and juice of 1 lemon
1 tablespoon honey

For the blintzes:
2 cups pot cheese (page 22)
1 teaspoon pure vanilla extract
½ teaspoon ground cinnamon
1 tablespoon granulated sugar
pinch of ground nutmeg
16 crêpes (page 27)

~To prepare the compote, combine 1 cup of the blueberries, lemon zest and juice, and honey in a small saucepan over medium heat. Simmer until the berries are soft and release their juices, 5 to 6 minutes. Transfer the cooked berries to a blender or a food processor fitted with a metal blade and purée until smooth. Return the purée to the pan, add the remaining berries, and heat through over medium heat. Keep warm, or let cool, cover, chill, and serve cold.

~To prepare the blintzes, in a small bowl combine the pot cheese, vanilla extract, cinnamon, sugar, and nutmeg and stir to combine. Spoon 2 tablespoons of the cheese mixture onto one end of a crêpe. Fold the sides of the crepe over the filling, then fold up as if a burrito. Repeat this process with the remaining crêpes and cheese mixture.

~Just before serving, heat a small nonstick sauté pan or crêpe pan over medium heat. Spray lightly with a vegetable coating spray. Add 2 blintzes to the pan. Sear on each side to color lightly and to heat the filling. Remove the blintzes to an individual serving plate. Spoon ¼ cup of the warm or chilled compote over the blintzes. Repeat with the remaining blintzes and compote. Serve at once.

Per serving: 170 calories
2.9 grams fat ~ 15% calories from fat

Oatmeal-Chocolate Chip Cookies

~There is something comforting in the process of baking chocolate chip cookies, as the kitchen fills with the aroma of melting chocolate and the sweet scent of caramelized brown sugar and butter. This recipe is truly a marvel; it reduces the traditional amount of butter or margarine from 1 cup to 5 tablespoons. The margarine (which must be stick margarine, not whipped margarine) is melted and then combined with the sugars, rather than the more common practice of creaming the fat with the sugars. This method reduces the amount of air that is incorporated into the cookie batter, allowing the baker to use less fat and still end up with a moist cookie. Banana purée is also added for moisture, plus the ratio of oatmeal to flour is higher than in many oatmeal cookie recipes. The result is a soft, chewy cookie that lets the naturally nutty texture of oatmeal shine through. A big glass of cold milk is the ideal accompaniment.

Makes 3 dozen cookies

½ cup all-purpose flour
¼ teaspoon salt
1 teaspoon baking soda
1½ cups old-fashioned rolled oats
5 tablespoons low-calorie stick margarine
⅓ cup firmly packed light brown sugar
⅓ cup granulated sugar

½ cup puréed banana (about ½ large banana)
1 teaspoon pure vanilla extract
¼ cup semisweet chocolate chips or mini chocolate chips

~Preheat an oven to 350° F. Line a baking sheet with parchment paper.

~In a large bowl stir together the flour, salt, baking soda, and oats. Set aside. Melt the margarine in a small pot on the stove; do not allow it to brown. Or place it in a glass cup and melt in a microwave oven set on high for 50 seconds. Pour the margarine into a medium-sized mixing bowl and add the sugars, banana, and vanilla extract. Using a rubber spatula or a wooden spoon, stir until smooth.

~Add the wet ingredients to the dry ingredients and stir until the mixture forms a dough. Stir in the chocolate chips.

~Spoon the dough by level tablespoons onto the prepared baking sheet, spacing them about 1-inch apart. Bake the cookies on the middle rack of the preheated oven until lightly puffed and golden, 8 to 10 minutes. They should be a little soft, but not too squishy in the center. Remove from the oven and transfer to wire racks. They will firm up further as they cool. Serve the cookies warm or cool.

Per cookie: 50 calories
1.5 grams fat ~ 27% calories from fat

Pear Butter Pound Cake

~Similar in method to pumpkin gingerbread (page 52), but with a much different final result: lightly spongy with a subtle pear flavor. Sprinkle slices of this moist, delicately flavored cake with confectioners' sugar and serve with citrus tea.

Makes 16 servings

¾ cup pear butter (page 23) or pear purée (see note)
1 cup nonfat vanilla yogurt
3 eggs
¾ cup granulated sugar
2 teaspoons pure vanilla extract
grated zest of 1 lemon
1½ cups cake flour
½ teaspoon baking soda
½ teaspoon baking powder
¼ teaspoon salt
¼ teaspoon ground cloves
¼ teaspoon ground nutmeg
½ teaspoon ground cinnamon

~Preheat an oven to 350° F. Spray an 8-cup bundt cake or tube pan lightly with a vegetable coating spray.

~In a small bowl whisk together the pear butter or pear purée and the yogurt. Set aside. In a separate bowl combine the eggs and sugar and beat with a mixer set on high speed until thickened and a light

(continued on page 68)

Chocolate Conclusions

C*hocolate, that alluring aristocrat of the dessert world—lush and welcoming in flavor yet forbidding in fat content—has sabotaged more than one diet. Yet no other food claims such ardent devotees. Self-proclaimed choc-oholics carry on an all-consuming love affair with their favorite flavor, be it meltingly sweet, smoothly seductive milk chocolate or rich, dark, intense bittersweet chocolate. Consumption can escalate to almost lethal doses.*

~*Despite its diet-defeating reputation, choco-late fanatics need not be banished to a choco-late-poor purgatory. Cocoa powder delivers the rich flavor chocolate addicts crave with the least amount of fat possible. These recipes encompass a wide variety of chocolate desserts, from a moist, fudgy chocolate génoise to a smooth, icy bittersweet chocolate sorbet.*

~*Few foods need to be completely eliminated from a low-fat diet and chocolate is no excep-tion. If carefully prepared, many chocolate desserts can be enjoyed on a low-calorie, low-fat regime. Few sensual pleasures can compete with the soul-satisfying taste of chocolate. Now you can have your cake and eat it, too.*

Chocolate Seashells

~The cocoa fudge sauce pulls double-duty in these sinfully chocolatey little cakes. It stands in for the melted semisweet or un-sweetened chocolate found in many choco-late batter cakes and it imparts a moist texture that butter or shortening would normally contribute. To create the seashell effect, split each cake in half horizontally and prop open with a small ball of vanilla ice milk or frozen yogurt. The rich choco-late flavor of these seashells is enhanced with tangy cranberry coulis (page 24) or strawberry coulis (page 24).

Makes 3 dozen small cakes

1½ cups cake flour
½ cup cocoa powder (not Dutch-process type)
1½ teaspoons baking soda
⅛ teaspoon salt
½ cup apple juice
1 tablespoon instant coffee powder
2 eggs
¾ cup vanilla sugar (page 21) or plain granulated sugar
1 teaspoon pure vanilla extract
1 teaspoon pure chocolate extract
¾ cup cocoa fudge sauce (page 25)
confectioners' sugar for topping (optional)

~Preheat an oven to 350° F. Spray three 12-well madeleine tins lightly with a vegetable coating spray.

~Sift together the flour, cocoa, baking soda, and salt into a bowl. Set aside. In a small saucepan heat the apple juice and dissolve the coffee powder in it. Set aside.

~Combine the eggs and sugar in another bowl and beat with a mixer set on high speed until thick and lemon colored, 2 to 3 minutes. Add the vanilla and chocolate extracts and continue beating until the eggs double in volume, about 5 minutes. Reduce the speed to low and gradually add the cocoa fudge sauce, beating just until combined. Alternately add the coffee-apple liquid and the flour mixture to the batter, beginning and ending with the liquid.

~Spoon the batter into the prepared molds, filling them two-thirds full. Bake the small cakes in the preheated oven until puffed and the tops spring back when touched lightly, 8 to 12 minutes. Be careful not to overbake. Remove from the oven and turn out onto wire racks to cool com-pletely. Sieve confectioners' sugar over the tops, if desired. Seashells that are not served immediately can be frozen successfully, if well-wrapped, for 1 month. Thaw at room temperature and dust with confectioners' sugar, if using, just before serving.

Per cake: 58 calories
0.6 grams fat ~ 9% calories from fat

Chocolate Génoise

~This moist fudgy cake weighs in with a miraculously low 1.8 grams of fat per serving. It is delicious sprinkled with confectioners' sugar and served with a fresh berry compote or in a pool of tart raspberry coulis.

Makes 16 servings

⅔ cup firmly packed Dutch-process cocoa
  powder
1 teaspoon instant coffee powder
⅔ cup water, boiling
1 teaspoon pure vanilla extract
4 egg yolks
1 cup vanilla sugar (page 21) or plain
  granulated sugar
6 egg whites, at room temperature
¾ cup cake flour, sifted twice
pinch of salt

~Preheat an oven to 350° F. Line the bottom of a 10-inch springform pan with parchment paper and spray lightly with a vegetable coating spray.

~Place the cocoa powder and instant coffee powder in a small bowl. Pour the boiling water over the cocoa powder and coffee and whisk gently to dissolve. Whisk in the vanilla extract. Set aside to cool.

~Combine the egg yolks and ½ cup of the sugar in a large metal or other heatproof bowl. Place the bowl in a large sauté pan filled halfway with simmering water and whisk continuously until the sugar crystals are dissolved and the mixture thickens and is warm to the touch, about 2 minutes. Be careful when heating the egg yolks, as they will scramble if left unattended or if they become too hot. Remove the bowl from the water and beat the yolk mixture with the whisk attachment of a mixer set on high speed until it doubles in volume and the bowl is cool to the touch, 3 to 5 minutes. Using a balloon whisk or a large rubber spatula, fold the cocoa mixture into the yolk mixture.

~Place the egg whites in a large, grease-free bowl. Using a mixer set at medium speed, beat until foamy. Increase the speed to high and beat until soft peaks form. Add the remaining ½ cup sugar, 1 tablespoon at a time, and continue beating until stiff, glossy peaks form.

~Sift the cake flour and the salt together and, using a balloon whisk or a large rubber spatula, gently fold it into the cocoa mixture. Then fold one third of the egg whites into the batter to lighten it. Finally, gently fold in the remaining egg whites.

~ Spoon the batter into the prepared pan. Bake the cake in the preheated oven until puffed and firm and the top springs back to the touch, or until a thin wooden skewer

inserted in the center comes out clean, 18 to 25 minutes. Be careful not to overbake. Remove from the oven and let cool for about 5 minutes on a wire rack. Remove the pan sides and slide the cooled cake off the pan bottom. Peel the parchment paper from the bottom of the cake and cool completely. Cut into slices to serve, or wrap the cooled cake well and freeze for up to 1 month.

Per serving: 97 calories
1.8 grams fat ~ 17% calories from fat

Hot Chocolate

~The British call it "nursery food"; to Americans, it is "comfort food." These are dishes that conjure up pleasant childhood memories of simple needs satisfied by simple foods. Hot chocolate, an old favorite and the most simple comfort food around, is perfect to sip slowly while curled up in your toasty flannel pajamas. This recipe is especially flavorful if the cocoa fudge sauce is made with vanilla-scented sugar syrup.

Makes 1 serving

1 cup nonfat milk
1 teaspoon pure vanilla extract
1 teaspoon pure chocolate extract
1 tablespoon plus 2 teaspoons cocoa fudge sauce (page 25)

~Combine the milk and the vanilla and chocolate extracts in a small saucepan and bring just to a boil. Spoon the cocoa fudge sauce into a mug and whisk in the hot milk mixture. Serve immediately.

~If you own an espresso machine, steam all the ingredients together to create a creamier, frothier drink.

Per serving: 150 calories
0.9 grams fat ~ 5% calories from fat

Mocha Lace Cookies

~These thin, coffee-flavored crisps are a variation on the traditional brandy snap. They make a great accompaniment to after-dinner coffee drinks, or, if molded into small cookie baskets, can hold a variety of fresh fruits, ice creams, or sorbets.

Makes 15 to 18 cookies

¼ cup all-purpose flour
1 tablespoon Dutch-process cocoa powder
2 tablespoons unsalted butter or margarine
2 tablespoons granulated sugar
2 tablespoons light corn syrup
1 teaspoon honey
½ teaspoon instant coffee granules
2 tablespoons brandy or dark Jamaican rum

~Preheat oven to 375° F. Line 2 baking sheets with parchment paper.

~Sift the flour and cocoa powder together into a bowl. Set aside. In a small saucepan combine the butter or margarine, sugar, corn syrup, honey, instant coffee, and brandy or rum. Place over medium heat and stir until the butter melts. Increase the heat to high and bring the mixture to a rolling boil. Remove from the heat and whisk in the flour-cocoa mixture.

~Spoon the batter, by level teaspoonfuls, onto the prepared baking sheets, spacing them at least 2 inches apart as these cookies will spread as they bake. It is usually possible to bake only 3 or 4 cookies on each sheet. Bake the cookies in the preheated oven until they spread thin and have a lacy appearance, 4 to 5 minutes.

~Remove from the oven and let cool for a few seconds. While still pliable, mold the cookies into tuiles by draping them over a rolling pin or bottle to cool. Alternatively, shape them into baskets by molding them around the bottom of small juice glasses, or into cigarettes by rolling them tightly around the handle of a wooden spoon or a small wooden dowel. The cookies will become very crisp as they cool. Bake the remaining cookie batter in the same way.

Per cookie: 36 calories
1.3 grams fat ~ 32% calories from fat

Chocolate Bread Pudding

~A classic American dessert becomes wonderfully self-indulgent when spiked with good-quality cocoa and a shot of brandy or Kahlúa. Let the bread become completely soaked with the chocolate custard before baking. Vanilla bean crème anglaise (page 25) is a good accompaniment.

Makes 8 servings

12 slices good-quality, day-old French or
*   Italian baguette, about 1-inch thick*
*   (3 or 4 ounces total weight)*
3 eggs
2½ cups nonfat milk
¼ cup honey
¼ cup granulated sugar
1 teaspoon pure vanilla extract
2 tablespoons brandy or Kahlúa
⅓ cup Dutch-process cocoa powder
2 teaspoons cornstarch
pinch of salt

~Preheat an oven to 325° F. Arrange the bread slices, staggering them, in a 12- or 14-inch-long oval gratin dish or a 4-cup soufflé dish.

~In a large bowl whisk together the eggs, milk, honey, sugar, vanilla and brandy or Kahlúa. Sift the cocoa powder, cornstarch, and salt together onto the egg mixture, then whisk until thoroughly combined.

~Pour the cocoa-egg mixture evenly over the bread slices and let stand until all of the bread is thoroughly saturated with the custard. Depending upon the freshness of the bread and the dish you choose, this could take 1 to 2 hours.

~Bake the pudding in the preheated oven until it is barely firm to the touch but not dry and pulling away from the sides of the dish, 40 to 60 minutes. Serve warm or, alternatively, cover and chill thoroughly before serving.

Per serving: 170 calories
2.7 grams fat ~ 14% calories from fat

Mexican Chocolate Angel Food Cake

~Lightly spicy, with a subtle chocolatey flavor, this angel food cake captures the essence of delicious Mexican desserts.

Makes 12 servings

2 teaspoons instant coffee granules
1 teaspoon pure vanilla extract
½ teaspoon pure almond extract
½ cup cocoa fudge sauce (page 25)
1 cup vanilla sugar (page 21)
¾ cup sifted cake flour
1 teaspoon ground cinnamon
14 egg whites, at room temperature
¼ teaspoon salt
1 teaspoon cream of tartar
confectioners' sugar for topping (optional)

~Preheat an oven to 350° F. In a small bowl, dissolve the coffee granules in the vanilla and almond extracts. Stir in the cocoa fudge sauce and set aside.

~In a food processor fitted with a metal blade, process 1 cup vanilla sugar for 1 or 2 minutes to create a finer grain. Sift the cake flour, cinnamon, and ½ cup of the vanilla sugar together twice into a large bowl. Set aside.

~Place the egg whites in a large, grease-free mixing bowl. Using a mixer set on medium speed, beat the egg whites until frothy. Increase the speed to high, add the salt and the cream of tartar, and continue beating until soft peaks form. Add the remaining ½ cup vanilla sugar, 1 table-spoon at a time, and continue beating until stiff, glossy peaks form. Sift one third of the flour mixture onto the egg whites. Using a balloon whisk or large rubber spatula, fold in gently. Repeat this process two more times with the remaining flour mixture.

~Using the whisk or spatula, stir a large spoonful of the egg white mixture into the cocoa fudge sauce to lighten it. Then care-fully fold the cocoa mixture into the egg white mixture, just until combined. Do not overmix.

~Spoon the batter into an ungreased 10-inch tube pan. Run a butter knife or thin metal spatula lightly through the batter to break up any air pockets. Bake the cake in the preheated oven until a thin wooden skewer inserted in the center comes out clean, 45 to 50 minutes. Remove from the oven and invert the cake onto a wire rack; do not remove the pan. Let cool completely, about 1 hour. When the cake is cool, turn it upright and run a thin metal spatula around the edge of the cake. Invert the cake onto a serving plate and lift off the pan. Just before serving, sieve confectioners' sugar over the top.

Per serving: 122 calories
.25 grams fat ~ 3% calories from fat

Bittersweet Chocolate Sorbet

~Intensely flavored, like a sophisticated Fudgesicle. The addition of liqueur gives this sorbet an adult edge and keeps it smooth through extended periods in the freezer—if it lasts that long!

Makes 8 servings

1 cup granulated sugar
⅔ cup firmly packed Dutch-process cocoa powder
1½ cups water
1 teaspoon pure vanilla extract
2 tablespoons Kahlúa, brandy, dark Jamaican rum, crème de menthe, Grand Marnier, or Framboise

~Combine the sugar and cocoa powder in a heavy-bottomed saucepan. Gradually mix in the water. Place over medium heat, bring to a simmer, and stir until the sugar dissolves. Increase the heat and bring to a boil. Boil the syrup until it is a dark, glossy brown, 1 to 2 minutes. Pour the mixture into a bowl and stir in the vanilla extract and liqueur of choice. Cover and chill until very cold.

~Pour the chocolate sorbet mixture into an ice cream maker and freeze according to the manufacturer's directions. Serve the sorbet immediately or transfer it to a 1-pint container, cover tightly, and freeze. Remove the frozen sorbet from the freezer and temper it in the refrigerator for 30 minutes before scooping. Alternatively, soften it in a microwave oven set on high for 40 to 60 seconds.

Per serving: 130 calories
0.8 grams fat ~ 6% calories from fat

Chocolate-Orange Biscotti

~Scented delicately with orange and very chocolatey, these crisp cookies are a perfect snack with an espresso or as dessert with sorbet and fresh fruit. The addition of almonds is optional, although they give the biscotti an appealing crunch and an attractive appearance.

Makes about 3 dozen cookies

⅓ cup (about 1 ounce) raw almonds (optional)
1 orange
2 eggs
2 tablespoons canola oil or safflower oil
1 teaspoon pure vanilla extract
¾ cup granulated sugar
1½ cups all-purpose flour
⅓ cup firmly packed Dutch-process cocoa powder
1 teaspoon baking powder
¼ teaspoon salt

~Preheat an oven to 350° F. Spray a baking sheet lightly with a vegetable coating spray.

~If using almonds, arrange them in a single layer on another baking sheet and toast in the preheated oven until lightly toasted and fragrant, about 5 minutes. Remove from the oven and let cool completely.

~Using a vegetable peeler remove the orange zest from the orange, being careful not to remove the bitter white pith with it. Dice the zest and place in a small bowl. Squeeze the juice from the orange into the bowl with the zest and then add the eggs, oil, and vanilla extract and mix well. In another, larger bowl, sift together the sugar, flour, cocoa powder, baking powder, and salt. Make a well in the center of the dry ingredients and pour the egg mixture into it. Stir the ingredients together with a spoon until completely combined. Gently knead in the almonds, if using. The dough should be firm but a little sticky. Enclose the dough in plastic wrap and chill for at least 1 hour or as long as overnight.

~Divide the dough in half. On a lightly floured work surface, use the palms of your hands to roll each section into a 9- or 10-inch log. Place the logs at least 3 inches apart on the prepared baking sheet.

~Bake in the preheated oven until the logs crack slightly down the center and are firm enough to slice but not hard, 35 to 45 minutes. Remove from the oven and reduce the temperature to 250° F. Remove the logs from the baking sheet to a cutting board. Using a sharp, serrated bread knife, slice each log on the diagonal into eighteen 1/2-inch-thick slices. Place the slices, cut side down, on the baking sheet and return to the oven. Bake until the slices are crisp, 20 to 25 minutes. Let cool completely before serving.

~Since the cookies are quite crisp, they have a long shelf life. Store them for 2 weeks or longer in a tightly covered container at room temperature.

Per cookie with almonds: 55 calories
1.8 grams fat ~ 28% calories from fat

Per cookie without almonds: 45 calories
1.1 grams fat ~ 20% calories from fat

Chocolate-Rum Zuccoto

~An unusual and beautiful dessert that is ideal for special occasions and is successfully made in advance. Any of the suggested liqueurs blend well with chocolate. If you decide to use Grand Marnier, add the grated zest of an orange with the cocoa powder to enhance the flavor. Serve slices of the zuccoto with vanilla bean crème anglaise (page 25) and a complementary coulis (page 24).

Makes 10 servings

1 recipe chocolate génoise (page 75)
2 teaspoons unflavored powdered gelatin
¼ cup dark Jamaican rum, brandy, Kahlúa, or Grand Marnier
⅓ cup cocoa powder (not Dutch-process type)
1 cup vanilla sugar (page 21) or plain granulated sugar
½ cup brewed coffee or water
2 whole eggs, separated, plus 2 egg whites
1 cup pot cheese (page 22)
1 teaspoon pure vanilla extract
1 teaspoon pure chocolate extract
cocoa powder and confectioners' sugar for topping

~Bake the *génoise* and let cool completely.

~Pour the rum, brandy, or liqueur into a small saucepan. Sprinkle the gelatin over it and let soften for about 5 minutes.

~Line a 4- or 5-cup metal or glass bowl with plastic wrap, pressing the wrap securely against the sides of the bowl.

~Using a long, sharp serrated knife, cut a ¼-inch-thick horizontal slice from the top of the chocolate *génoise* . Set aside. Carefully slice six or seven ¼-inch-thick vertical strips from the *génoise* (about one fourth of the cake). Without overlapping, lay the cake strips tightly against each other in the bowl, making sure the entire surface of the bowl is covered with cake. If needed, fit smaller strips of cake into areas of the bowl that the larger strips do not cover. Reserve remaining uncut *génoise* for another use.

~In a heavy-bottomed, noncorrosive saucepan, combine the cocoa powder, ½ cup of the granulated sugar, coffee or water, egg yolks and the softened gelatin. Whisk together over low heat until smooth. Increase the heat slightly and stir constantly until the mixture thickens enough to coat the back of a spoon. Do not let the mixture boil or it may curdle. Remove from the heat and let cool slightly.

~Stir the pot cheese into the cocoa mixture. Chill until cold and just beginning to set, 10 to 15 minutes. Stir in the vanilla and chocolate extracts.

~While the cocoa mixture is chilling, prepare the egg whites. In a large metal or other heatproof bowl, combine 4 egg whites with the remaining ½ cup sugar. Place the bowl in a sauté pan filled halfway with simmering water and whisk continuously until the sugar crystals dissolve and the mixture is hot to the touch (120° F), 3 to 4 minutes. Remove the bowl from the

water and beat the egg mixture with the whisk attachment of a mixer set on high speed until it triples in volume and the bowl is cool to the touch, about 5 minutes. Using a balloon whisk or a large rubber spatula, fold one third of the egg whites into the chilled cocoa mixture to lighten it. Then gently fold in the remaining egg whites. Spoon the mixture into the cake-lined bowl and top with the reserved cake round. Trim the cake round to fit snugly inside the bowl. Cover with plastic wrap and chill until firm, 4 to 6 hours.

~To serve, uncover the bowl and invert onto a serving platter. Lift off the bowl and peel off the plastic wrap. Sieve cocoa powder over the top and sieve confectioners' sugar over the cocoa powder. Serve immediately or chill until serving.

Per serving: 178 calories
2.46 grams fat ~ 12% calories from fat

Cappuccino Fudge Roulade

~Much of the preflavored nonfat frozen yogurt or ice milk on the market tastes bland or artificial. Flavoring these products yourself is the only way to create deliciously intense, true flavors. Beating frozen yogurt or ice milk with a mixer aerates it and makes it creamier and less icy— closer in texture to premium ice creams.

Makes 12 servings

For the chocolate génoise:

⅔ cup cake flour

⅓ cup Dutch process cocoa powder

¼ teaspoon salt

4 eggs

½ cup granulated sugar

1 teaspoon pure vanilla extract

2 tablespoons Dutch-process cocoa powder
   mixed with 2 tablespoons confectioners'
   sugar

For the cappuccino filling:

¼ cup instant coffee granules

2 tablespoons brewed coffee

2 tablespoons Kahlúa

1 quart nonfat vanilla frozen yogurt or
   ice milk

1 tablespoon espresso-roast coffee beans,
   ground to a powder (optional)

~Preheat an oven to 350° F. Line a 9-by-13-inch roulade, or jelly-roll pan with parchment paper and spray lightly with a vegetable coating spray.

~To prepare the cake, sift the flour, cocoa, and salt together twice into a bowl. Set aside.

~Combine the eggs and sugar in a large metal or other heatproof bowl. Place the bowl in a sauté pan filled halfway with simmering water and whisk continuously until the sugar crystals dissolve and the mixture is hot to the touch (120° F), 3 to 4 minutes. Remove the bowl from the water and beat the egg mixture with the whisk attachment of a mixer set on high speed until it triples in volume and the bowl is cool to the touch, about 5 minutes. Whisk in the vanilla extract. Using a balloon whisk, or a large rubber spatula, gently fold the flour mixture into the batter, one third at a time.

~Spread the batter in the prepared pan. Bake the cake in the preheated oven until puffed and firm to the touch but not dry, 12 to 15 minutes. Meanwhile, lay a piece of parchment paper or a thin cotton dish towel the same dimensions as the *génoise* on a flat surface. Sprinkle lightly with the remaining cocoa-sugar mixture. Remove the cake from the oven and invert it onto the parchment paper or the dish towel. Peel off the parchment the cake was baked on.

Roll up the warm cake, including the parchment or dish towel it is laid on, like a jelly roll. Let cool completely before unrolling and filling.

~While the cake is cooling, prepare the cappuccino filling. In a small bowl stir together the coffee granules, the brewed coffee, and the Kahlúa until the coffee granules dissolve and the mixture is smooth and syrupy. In a large bowl combine the frozen yogurt and coffee syrup and beat with a mixer set on low to medium speed until smooth and spreadable, but still frozen. Stir in the ground coffee, if desired. If the filling seems too soft, slip it into the freezer until it is almost completely firm.

~Unroll the cake and spread the cappuccino filling over the surface. Roll up again like a jelly roll, this time without the parchment paper or towel. Wrap tightly in plastic wrap and then in aluminum foil and freeze until firm. Keep frozen until ready to serve.

~Slice the roulade when it is still frozen solid and let the slices soften slightly before serving.

Per serving: 150 calories
2 grams fat ~ 12% calories from fat

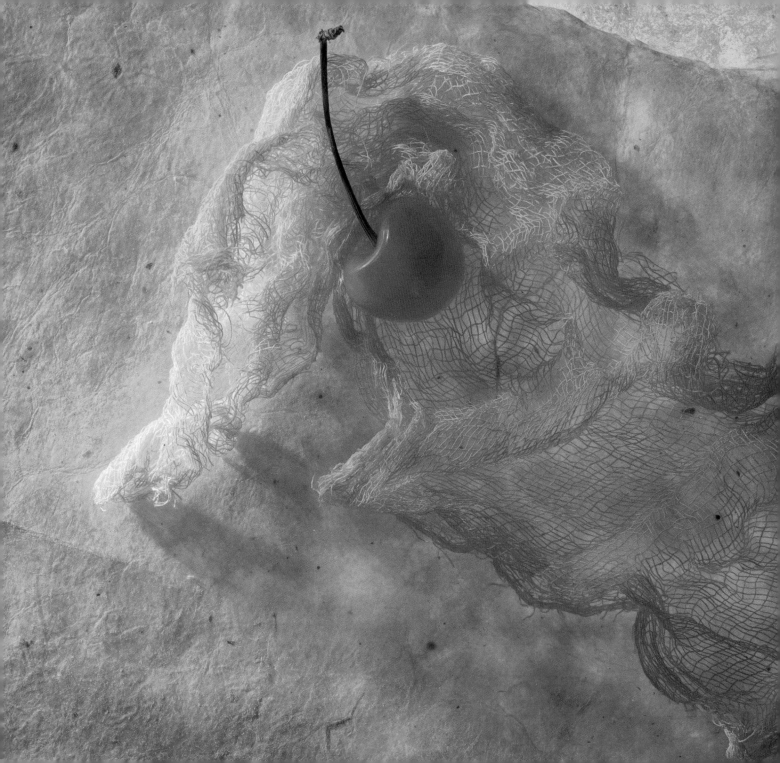

Light Finishes

*L*ight in taste and easy to make, these desserts take advantage of the full, lush flavors of ripe seasonal fruits and enhance them with a splash of liqueur, a little champagne or a sprinkling of sweet herbs. Fast, simple, and beautiful to serve, they are short on ingredients but not on taste—an ideal finish to a large or spicy meal, or the perfect sweet finale when even one gram of fat is too much.

~These are the recipes to turn to when you are not in the mood to do serious baking, but still want something special. The shakes, compotes, and fruit sorbets in this chapter are the answers to those cravings that items from the supermarket frozen food section can never satisfy.

Melon with Essencia and Fresh Mint

~This dessert is also delicious served for breakfast or brunch, with or without the addition of Essencia, the sweet dessert wine made from muscat grapes. Remember to be gentle when shredding the mint; it bruises easily and will turn black.

Makes 8 servings

4 cups cantaloupe melon balls
4 cups honeydew melon balls
2 cups freshly squeezed orange juice
1 cup Essencia dessert wine
¼ cup loosely packed fresh mint leaves,
    shredded into a fine chiffonade
8 sprigs fresh mint for garnish

~Combine the melon balls, orange juice, and wine in a large bowl. Toss lightly, cover, and chill for 30 to 60 minutes.

~Just before serving, add the shredded mint to the melon mixture and toss gently. Divide the fruit and marinade among 8 dessert glasses. Garnish each glass with a mint sprig. Serve immediately.

Per serving: 110 calories
0 grams fat ~ 0% calories from fat

Strawberries Mimosa

~Refreshing, luxurious, and incredibly easy.

Makes 8 servings

4 cups (2 pints) strawberries, hulled and sliced lengthwise
¼ cup Grand Marnier
½ cup freshly squeezed orange juice or tangerine juice
1 tablespoon granulated sugar (optional)
2 cups champagne

~In a large bowl combine the strawberries, Grand Marnier, and citrus juice. Add the sugar if the berries are not sweet enough and then mix gently. Cover and chill for 30 minutes. Do not marinate much longer, as the berries will start to become mushy.

~Spoon the marinated berries into 8 champagne flutes. Pour ¼ cup champagne over each flute of berries. Serve immediately.

Per serving: 95 calories
0 grams fat ~ 0% calories from fat

Pineapple with Kiwi Salsa

~Light and refreshing and stylish enough to serve after a spicy company dinner. Use ripe but firm kiwifruits to avoid a watery salsa. If a more substantial dessert is desired, spoon a small scoop of vanilla frozen yogurt or tropical-flavored sorbet into the center of the pineapple ring before topping with the kiwi salsa.

Makes 8 servings

1 pineapple
1 cup vanilla sugar syrup (page 22)
1 barely ripe banana
4 to 5 ripe but firm kiwifruits
2 tablespoons dark Jamaican rum
1 tablespoon freshly squeezed lime juice
grated zest of 1 orange (optional)

~Using a sharp knife, carefully slice off the top and bottom of the pineapple. Pare the rind from the pineapple; try to remove the eyes with the rind without removing too much of the flesh. Slice the pineapple crosswise into 8 round slices. Using a small, round cookie or biscuit cutter or a sharp paring knife, remove the center core from each pineapple round (you will end up with the familiar pineapple "ring").

~In a large sauté pan, bring the vanilla syrup to a simmer over medium heat. Add the pineapple rings to the warm syrup, cover, and remove from the heat. Let the pineapple rings soak in the syrup until the syrup is cool, about 10 minutes. Refrigerate the pineapple in the syrup until it is very cold, at least 1 to 2 hours.

~While the pineapple is chilling, prepare the salsa. Peel and dice the banana into ⅛- to ¼-inch chunks. Place in a bowl. Peel and dice the kiwifruits into the same-size chunks as the banana and add to the bowl. Add the rum, lime juice, and the orange zest, if desired, and toss gently. Cover and chill until ready to serve.

~Using a slotted utensil, remove the pineapple from the syrup, draining well. There will be about ¾ cup syrup left; strain the syrup and keep it in a covered container in the refrigerator for another use.

~Place 1 pineapple slice on each individual serving plate. Spoon a mound of the kiwi salsa into the center of each pineapple ring. Serve immediately.

Per serving: 100 calories
0 grams fat ~ 0% calories from fat

Blackberry-Cabernet Sorbet

~The flavor of this garnet-colored sorbet will only be as good as the wine you choose. A fruity Beaujolais Nouveau would work well, too.

Makes 8 servings

1 pound frozen unsweetened blackberries, thawed
½ cup Cabernet Sauvignon or other good-quality red wine
¼ cup granulated sugar

~Place the thawed berries and any accumulated juice in a food processor fitted with a metal blade or in a blender and purée until smooth. To remove the seeds, press the puréed berries through a fine-mesh sieve held over a bowl; discard the seeds. You should have about 2 cups purée.

~Combine the wine and sugar in a small, noncorrosive saucepan. Place over medium heat, bring to a simmer, and cook, stirring, just until the sugar dissolves. Pour the wine syrup into a small bowl and let cool completely.

~Add the wine syrup to the berry purée, stir well, cover, and chill until very cold. Place the chilled berry mixture in an ice cream maker and freeze according to the manufacturer's directions.

~Serve the sorbet immediately, or store in a covered container in the freezer for up to 1 month. If serving the sorbet from the freezer, temper it in the refrigerator for 20 minutes before scooping, or soften it in a microwave oven set on high for 40 to 60 seconds.

Per serving: 70 calories
0 grams fat ~ 0% calories from fat

Mango-Cardamom Sorbet

~Cardamom adds a distinctively sweet taste and unusual fragrance to the tropical mango. Full of vitamins A and C and loaded with fiber, the mango makes a healthy and delicious dessert choice.

Makes 8 servings

3 large mangoes
¼ cup plain sugar syrup (page 22), or to taste
¼ cup freshly squeezed lime juice, or to taste
¼ teaspoon ground cardamom, or to taste

~Peel the mangoes and carefully cut the flesh away from the stones. Place the flesh in a food processor fitted with a metal blade or in a blender. Using your fingertips squeeze any additional juices or flesh away from the stone, into the processor or blender. Purée until smooth. You should have about 2 cups purée. Add the sugar syrup, the lime juice, and the cardamom and stir to combine. Taste the mixture at this point. If it seems too sweet, add a little more lime juice, 1 teaspoon at a time. If it is too tart, add a little more sugar syrup, 1 teaspoon at a time. If you prefer a more pronounced cardamom taste, add a pinch or two more at this point. Remember, cardamom is a strong spice and will become more pronounced after the sorbet is frozen and has a chance to "age." I find this sorbet is most successful when the spice is subtle. Cover and chill until very cold. Place the chilled mango mixture in an ice cream maker and freeze according to the manufacturer's directions.

~Serve the sorbet immediately, or store in a covered container in the freezer for up to 1 month. If serving the sorbet from the freezer, temper it in the refrigerator for 20 minutes before scooping, or soften it in a microwave oven set on high for 40 to 60 seconds.

Per serving: 70 calories
0 grams fat ~ 0% calories from fat

Raspberry-Champagne Sorbet

~Crisp, elegant, and bursting with berry flavor.

Makes 8 servings

1 pound unsweetened frozen raspberries, thawed
¼ cup plain sugar syrup (page 22)
½ cup champagne or other sparkling wine

~Place the berries and any accumulated juices in a food processor fitted with a metal blade or in a blender and purée. To remove the seeds, press the puréed berries through a fine-mesh sieve held over a bowl; discard the seeds. You should have about 2 cups purée.

~Add the sugar syrup and the champagne to the berry purée, stir well, cover, and chill until very cold. Place the chilled berry mixture in an ice cream maker and freeze according to the manufacturer's directions.

~Serve the sorbet immediately, or store in a covered container in the freezer for up to 1 month. If serving the sorbet from the freezer, temper it in the refrigerator for 20 minutes before scooping, or soften it in a microwave oven set on high for 40 to 60 seconds.

Per serving: 55 calories
0 grams fat ~ 0% calories from fat

Tropical Fruit Smoothie

~This fruity drink is familiar to anyone who has visited their local yogurt stand. Whip one up at home and save time—and a few calories. You can use frozen strawberries, peaches, or nectarines instead of the banana to thicken the smoothie, or substitute a host of other fruits for the tropical ones listed. Smoothies make a great dessert, snack, or quick breakfast. Serve in a frosted goblet and garnish with a small skewer of fresh fruit.

Makes 2 servings

½ cup fresh pineapple chunks or drained pineapple chunks canned in their juice, chilled
½ cup pineapple juice, chilled
½ ripe papaya, peeled, seeded, and cut into chunks
½ cup nonfat banana, vanilla, or plain yogurt
1 banana, cut into 1-inch chunks and frozen solid
2 small skewers fresh fruit for garnish (optional)

~Combine the pineapple chunks and juice, papaya, and yogurt in a blender and blend until smooth. Add the banana chunks, one at a time, and blend until thick, smooth, and creamy. Pour into frosted goblets and garnish with the fruit skewers, if desired. Serve immediately.

Per serving: 133 calories
0 grams fat ~ 0% calories from fat

Raspberry-Lemon Parfait

~The lemon-flavored frozen yogurt here is tart and intense, rivaling the most fattening lemon ice creams in richness and flavor. Strawberry, kiwi, or peach coulis would work well in place of the raspberry coulis.

Makes 4 servings

1 pint nonfat vanilla frozen yogurt or ice milk
grated zest and juice of 1 large lemon
½ teaspoon pure lemon extract
1 cup raspberry coulis (page 24)
1 cup (½ pint) fresh raspberries
4 raspberries and 4 strips lemon zest for
*   garnish*

~If using hard-packed frozen yogurt or ice milk, combine it in a bowl with the grated lemon zest, juice, and lemon extract. Beat on medium speed using a hand-held mixer or a free-standing mixer fitted with a paddle attachment. (Beating hard-packed ice milk breaks up the ice crystals, giving it a texture closer to premium ice cream.) If using soft-serve frozen yogurt, simply stir in the lemon juice, zest, and extract by hand using a wooden spoon or balloon whisk. Return the flavored yogurt or ice milk to the freezer for at least 30 minutes for flavors to blend.

~To create parfaits, use 6-ounce champagne flutes, parfait, or decorative juice glasses. Spoon 2 tablespoons raspberry coulis into the bottom of each glass and top with 2 tablespoons of the raspberries. Spoon ¼ cup of the yogurt or ice milk over the raspberries. Spoon on an additional 2 tablespoons raspberry coulis and 2 tablespoons raspberries. Top each parfait with ¼ cup yogurt or ice milk. Garnish each serving with a fresh raspberry and a curl of lemon zest.

Per serving: 127 calories
0 grams fat ~ 0% calories from fat

Raspberry Brulée

~A quick way to dress up summer raspberries or any fragrant summer fruit or berry. Top the ramekins of fruit with honey-yogurt sauce and chill until ready to serve. Caramelize the brown sugar topping just before serving to keep it crisp. Invest in an inexpensive blow torch at your local hardware store to make the job extra easy, or slip the ramekins under a hot broiler.

Makes 8 servings

2 cups (1 pint) fresh raspberries
2 tablespoons Framboise or other berry-
*   flavored liqueur*
1½ to 2 cups honey-yogurt sauce (page 22)
8 tablespoons light brown sugar

~Place the berries in a large bowl, add the Framboise, and toss gently. Divide the berries among eight 2- or 3-ounce flame-proof ramekins or small custard cups. Carefully spoon 3 or 4 tablespoons of the honey yogurt sauce over each serving of berries, making sure the berries are completely covered. Cover and chill until ready to serve, up to 3 hours.

~A few minutes before serving, sieve 1 tablespoon brown sugar evenly over each ramekin of yogurt-covered berries. Set a blow torch at a medium flame and carefully caramelize the sugar with its flame. The sugar will become a crisp, shiny glaze. Alternatively, preheat a broiler and set the oven rack as close to the broiler as possible. Place the ramekins on a baking sheet and slide under the broiler. Position the door of the broiler ajar and broil the sugar topping until crisp and shiny, about 1 minute. Serve immediately.

Per serving: 110 calories
0 grams fat ~ 0% calories from fat

Citrus Granita

~If you do not want to buy the fruit and juice it yourself, try the freshly squeezed citrus juices available in the produce section of the supermarket. Do not use frozen juices, however, as the taste will be inferior.

Makes 8 servings

2 cups freshly squeezed tangerine juice
2½ cups freshly squeezed orange juice
1 cup freshly squeezed pink grapefruit juice
½ cup freshly squeezed lime juice
3 tablespoons Grand Marnier
2 or 3 tablespoons granulated sugar
   (optional)

~In a bowl stir together all the citrus juices and the Grand Marnier. If the juices are too tart, sweeten with the sugar as needed. Pour into a loaf pan and place in the freezer. Every 15 or 20 minutes, stir with a fork to break up the ice crystals. Freeze until firm.

~Just before serving, remove the loaf pan from the freezer. If the *granita* is frozen solid, dip the bottom of the pan in hot water to loosen it from the pan. Invert the pan onto a large cutting board and lift it off. Using a sharp French chef's knife, shave the *granita* into large slivers. Divide the slivers among 8 dessert glasses and serve immediately.

Per serving: 90 calories
0 grams fat ~ 0% calories from fat

Chocolate Monkey Milk Shake

~Most diet shakes are thickened with ice and then flavored, giving them a watery finish. This shake, however, is about as close to the real thing as you can get— thick, rich, and creamy. The frozen bananas give it both taste and texture without watering down the flavor. Make sure all the ingredients are cold and the bananas are frozen solid before putting them in the blender.

2 servings

1 cup nonfat milk
2 tablespoons nonfat milk powder
2 tablespoons cocoa fudge sauce (page 25)
1 teaspoon pure vanilla extract
1 teaspoon pure chocolate extract
1 banana, cut into 1-inch chunks and frozen
   solid

~Combine the milk, milk powder, cocoa fudge sauce, and vanilla and chocolate extracts in a blender and blend until smooth. Add the frozen banana chunks, one at a time, and blend until shake is smooth and thick. Pour into goblets and serve immediately.

Per serving: 150 calories
0.9 grams fat ~ 5.4% calories from fat

Index

{ I N D E X }

  flavored sugar, 21
  flavored sugar syrup, 22
  liquid sweeteners for, 17
  nutrition of, 20
  plain sugar syrup, 22
  role of, in baking, 17, 20
  substitutes for, 20
summer berry croustade, 68
syrups, 22

T

tangerine sugar, 21
tarts
  fresh apple, 58
  ruby pear, with poire Williams
    sabayon, 42, 44
tortes. *See* cakes
tropical fruit smoothie, 96
turnovers, apple and dried sour cherry,
  57-58

V

vanilla
  sugar, 21
  sugar syrup, 22
  vanilla bean crème anglaise, 25
vegetable coating spray, 20

Y

yogurt cheese, 23

Z

zuccoto, chocolate-rum, 84